THE BOOK I WISH I'D READ AT 13

Helping girls to love themselves

KELLY OAKES

Dear Emma

Enjoy the read!

Love

Kelly

Dedicated to the younger me, who suffered within.

For if I wasn't you then, I wouldn't be me now.

Contents

About the Author

Kelly Oakes is a 'normal' mum, wife, daughter and friend. After many years of self-hurt, and then triggered by the death of her dad and mum, she was forced onto a new path of self-discovery and self-healing.

Now 40, Kelly lives in Essex with her husband, Tom, and their two children, Ted and Kit. She started her working career as a marketeer and fundraiser for charities, which is still an important part of her life.

After a series of devastating life events, Kelly began looking for ways to manage debilitating anxiety, mainly relating to the safely and health of her children. This journey of self-help led Kelly to discover, among other things, meditation, journaling, daily rituals, breath work, the healing benefits of nature and the inspiration of books and podcasts.

The Book I Wish I'd Read at 13 is a curated library of the #FortyTools Kelly used to transform her life and her mental health.

She shares her story and journey to inspire others to heal themselves. As Kelly proves, it's never too late to find, nurture and love the true you.

Follow Kelly on Instagram:
@kellyoakes_x (personal)
@by_kellyoakes (professional)

Acknowledgements

There are many people I'd like to thank for helping me on my journey to writing this book, intentionally or unintentionally. Firstly, my parents. Except for the obvious role they played in bringing me into this world, they have shaped the person I have been and the person I am today.

I spent 30-35 years hurting myself without consciously realising it, a few years knowing what I was doing but carrying on anyway, and then another couple of years healing myself and righting the damage I had done. The battles I have fought throughout my years may have, in part, been because of decisions made by my parents in the early years of my life. But that's not to say they were to blame. They were both playing their game of life with the cards they had been dealt, and neither of them were given an easy hand.

Acknowledgements

Mum and Dad always had my best interests at heart. They were always working, fighting for, and protecting their family in the best way they knew how. The hurt came from how I spoke with myself, how I interpreted my own thoughts into feelings and then into actions. Damaging actions.

The hard days I have lived and the pain I have caused myself and others, I wouldn't change. I am the person I am now thanks to the person I was then.

My husband, Tom. You've been everything I have needed when I have needed it. You made me leave the house with our kids on days when it would have been easier to stay home. You've been the lively energy our children have needed when I have felt flat. You are dependable, always there when the kids and I need you. Mr Practical but also Mr Fun, you are kind, generous and loving. I'm proud of you for the journey you have been on, alongside my own. We've grown together and that's the sign of a strong marriage.

My friends, the girls, all of my girls, but especially Tasha, Vicky, Lisa and Anna. We're all different but together we make each other feel complete, a full set. You have never judged me or made me feel lonely, even when I have distanced myself socially. In 25 years of friendship, I've never argued with any of you and I hope I never do.

By me writing and you reading the words in this book, I hope we'll all feel even closer, connected and understood. I hope it gives you the permission, and bravery, to be your true selves with me too.

Our family, my side and Tom's. A whole bunch of personalities and a huge amount of love. As I've come to understand and love myself more, I understand and love you more too.

I feel guilty that I've hidden so much of myself from you. I can now be fully present in your company without being preoccupied with how awkward and inferior I used to feel.

I'm thankful to you all for trusting me, never questioning what I might write in this book, eagerly asking me when it will be published and when you can read it.

I'm nervous about your reaction to the side of me you'll discover when you read this for the first time but it's so freeing to know there will be no more hiding who I have been, just acceptance and love for who I am now.

Claire and Alexa, my publishing team, for holding my hand throughout this whole process. You've made it so easy for me to put my thoughts, feelings, emotions and discoveries into written words and printed pages.

Acknowledgements

My babies, Ted and Kit. Thank you for stopping me from feeling lonely. For showing me unconditional love and giving me purpose. I think you both saved my life.

I sit and watch you when you don't realise, taking in every part of you, every day. Watching you as you grow physically, emotionally, intelligently and in personality. You make my whole heart feel so full every time I see your faces, when you've been to sleep, been to school, even just when you've been in another room.

You brighten our days, and you make our lives so incredible, so perfect. I am grateful for you both. I promise to do the best job I can as your mum.

Finding me

Born in Ashford, Kent, on the 27 April 1980, I was the fourth child to my mum, Carol, aged 35, and the only child to my dad, John, aged 22.

Mum and Dad had been married for a year or so before I came along. I've been told I was conceived because my grandad, Titch, my dad's dad, was dying from emphysema and they wanted him to have a grandchild before he died.

He lovingly hand-crafted my cot and protectively waited at the crossroads near our home to make sure I arrived safely from my first journey from the hospital.

Mum already had three children from a previous marriage, to Roger. When I came along, Angela was 16, Mark was 15 and Tina was 13.

For as long as I can remember, I've grown up thinking I didn't fit in, that I wasn't good enough. Looking back, this has been the root cause of so much sadness and shame.

Even now, writing this book, a voice inside me asks: *Do people want to read your story? Is your 'story' even a story? Are you healed enough to be offering advice to other people?* The difference is that now I have the answers to reply to those voices.

Yes, people do want to hear my story and, yes, my story is a story worth sharing. Everyone has story. I have no doubt there are elements in this book that everyone can relate to. If I can help one person to love themselves, live life to the full and be more positive for the future, that's one life saved.

It's thanks to the many personal stories I have read and heard, from people baring their truth and experiences, that I have come to learn so much about myself.

Writing has been a transformative process, releasing internal pain and creating inner freedom and peace. Creating some space and light within my consciousness. Writing has been, and is, cathartic for me. I may not be the best writer – imposter syndrome has set in many times and told me I'm not cut out for writing a book, that my vocabulary isn't extensive enough to warrant it – but mental illness and trauma are not limited by class, education or intelligence. I'm sharing my story for anyone to read and I want it to be accessible.

If you have battled with a lack of self-worth, a feeling of not belonging, anxiety, an unhealthy relationship with food, a desire to be a better role-model for your children or future children, or even if you're just interested in reading other people's life experiences, I know you will take something away from this book – the book I wish I'd read at 13.

Following a childhood of fragile relationships, broken families and disordered eating from the age of three(ish), I spent thirty-seven years with no sense of belonging and no self-worth, and shame and blame by the bucket load. The feelings were tucked away, hidden from those around me, slowly corroding the edges of my soul like a rotten piece of fruit at the bottom of my handbag.

My teenage years mainly consisted of toxic, obsessive relationships, self-harm, drug use and a fully-fledged eating disorder, which would take grip for close to twenty years, peaking when I was five months pregnant with my son.

In August 2017, my walls began to collapse. My mum had a major, life-changing, stroke. She was hospitalised for five months.

She returned home, against the odds, paralysed, needing carers, and having to learn to eat, drink, swallow and talk again.

The day before she returned home, in January 2018, my dad died. I watched him take his last breath.

When he died, I was forced on to a new path. But was it to be a better one?

Later in the same year, I miscarried our third child, surrounded by our friends and family on the beach in Mykonos. Our two children had named their new baby sibling Wren or Ralphie and witnessing their grief remains the greatest challenge of my life.

I hit rock bottom. I was diagnosed with depression and anxiety disorder, referred for therapy, and put on anti-depressants. At the end of my initial consultation I was deemed 'not a priority' because I wasn't suicidal, although it had crossed my mind.

The anti-depressants rid me of all emotion, bad and good. I felt numb. Like I was just existing in life, not living.

Every day I woke up ashamed of my reflection. Weighed down by the secrets I'd been carrying around with me all my life, until now.

I'm high functioning, an achiever. This history of self-destruction, shame and self-harm has been a secret I've shared with only myself for forty years.

As I turn 40, I bare all. To be reborn.

Borne out of journaling, this book is an important part of my own recovery.

I am truly thankful for my life experiences, the bumps in the road. I'm at peace with the hard times I faced, and the negativity I carried around for so long. For it all shaped who I am now.

Every time I have made myself vulnerable, let down my wall of strength, I have been left feeling stronger. With steely determination, I awakened myself to the life I could lead. I bared all to be reborn, for myself as an individual and as a mother.

The Book I Wish I'd Read At 13 is proof that from adversity, real growth comes.

There will be elements in this book that everyone can relate to, whether mental health, self-harm, the weight of shame or blame, or what remains one of the greatest taboos – an eating disorder.

I'm an expert by experience, with a personal story to be told.

Books don't need to be read from cover to cover without stopping. I will often have two or three books on the go at any one time, dipping in and out depending on my mood. I'll fold corners, write notes and highlight sections. Books are the tools to help us navigate our lives.

You may have noticed this book has margins wide enough for you to add your notes, so grab yourself a cup of tea and a pencil and sit back and enjoy it. I hope you take something positive away from reading the pages that follow.

Birth to Rock-Bottom

Memories

I spent my first seven years growing up in Kent. Memories are few and far between. That's not to say my childhood was bad, I just remember it feeling…well, actually, I don't remember much.

When you force yourself to think back, one memory leads to another and those that do pop up are often random, unusual. Here are some of mine:

- My grandad worked on a farm and we'd been to his fields to see the new lambs. It was springtime, near to my third birthday, and I sat on the back seat of Dad's car and opened a 12-inch vinyl record of Culture Club's 'I'll Tumble for Ya'. This is still one of my favourite songs and makes me smile whenever I hear it.

- Waking up one morning and innocently going to the toilet in my little fluffy nighty, weighing myself and – at three stones – thinking I weighed too much. It's only now that I have my own children, who recently had to be weighed to be fitted for their skis, I realised I must have only been 3 or 4.

- I was so ashamed of my weight even then, before starting school. So much so I refused my early-years medical assessments. I kicked and screamed until they gave up on me. As a result, they didn't notice I had limited vision in one eye, until it was too late to correct. I lost my sight in my right eye.

- I can remember sitting on a rug in front of my parents' fireplace, my long, bouncy, blonde curls falling over my shoulders, counting the four rolls on my tummy, thinking I had to get rid of them. We moved from that house when I was 7 so I could only have been 5 or 6.

- I used to dread any school plays or reasons to dress up as I didn't think the costumes would fit me. In later years, the joy of being selected for a team would be quickly followed by the fear of trying on the team kit. I felt like the biggest, awkward person in any group. I just wanted to shrink myself.

- My parents used to manage petrol stations. Most evenings after school and during school holidays, I wandered around in the shop or in the office watching TV and playing games. Countless evenings after school I sat watching 'SuperTed' and 'The Raggy Dolls'. This was in the mid-80s and kids' TV was limited to 15:30-17:00. As I grew older, I filled the following hour or two with 'Blue Peter', 'Neighbours' and 'Home and Away'. Hugh Grant's character in the film 'About a Boy' describes filling his day with thirty-minute activities to make the day pass more quickly. I did the same thing whenever I wasn't at school. What a contrast to children nowadays who often can't sit without technology or stimulation to occupy their minds for longer than a few minutes.

- I would sneak food from the shop storeroom into the toilet and eat bars and bars of chocolate at a time. In case anyone found the wrappers, I would take a walk outside and hide them in the forecourt bins, pretending to be sweeping up.

- I remember walking to a local SPAR shop for penny sweets and using half-pennies to buy milk chocolate buttons and white chocolate fish.
- A memory flashes in my mind of holding a red salad bowl with a handle on the top, swirling a handful of lettuce leaves. I can still feel the resistance of the lettuce as it swirled against the plastic, like walking against a strong current in the sea.
- Fishing with my dad at a stream close to his house, with me grimacing as he warmed a fist full of maggots in his mouth.
- Waking up after the hurricane of 1987 and seeing the streets lined with fallen trees. I can still feel the panic as we drove to the petrol station my mum managed and saw the pole sign flattened to the floor, littered across the forecourt in pieces like autumn leaves.
- Fearfully crossing the train track to get to a traditional, large seesaw in our local park.
- A winter's day at work with my mum, when a car slid through the shop window and into the ice cream freezer I had just stepped away from.

I sit and wonder how significant it is that most of my memories are food or fear related.

When I was 7, my parents divorced. I was a daddy's girl and my mum told me I cried myself to sleep, every night, for six months.

No place like home

I moved several times between the ages of 7 to 15. You often hear people talk about their family home; well, I've never really had one. I've moved thirteen times in my life and can easily up sticks and move on without much looking back. I can love deeply but have developed the ability to disconnect and protect seamlessly, except in the case of my own children who I struggle to be away from for more than a few hours.

Soon after my parents separated, my mum, Tina and I moved from Kent to Essex.

Because Tina was older, and working, and I was still at school, I stayed behind in Kent for two months so Mum and Tina could get settled in the new home and business. I lived with my Auntie Ann, my dad's sister, and my cousins, and moved to their primary school.

Even now, looking back, this time makes me feel so sad and lonely. Not because I didn't love them but because I just felt so alone and different. An outcast.

Oddly, considering I was 7, my only real memory from those months is of learning about Mount Vesuvius in a creepy, dark school which was either a converted church, or made to look like one.

I don't blame Mum for leaving me behind.

She has her own story: a tough childhood of adoption, no-love, and some experiences she firmly says she will never share with us.

When Mum was in her twenties, married with three children on the Isle of Sheppey, she was talking with her then mother-in-law who let slip that Mum's parents were not her biological parents, that she was adopted. Mum had lost touch with the family who had brought her up, who she had been told were her mum and dad. She never felt as though she belonged. The news of adoption, I think, helped to explain why.

A few years ago, we traced Mum's family tree. She was born in March 1945, to Elsie. Elsie was married and had two older children. Her husband was away serving in the Second World War when Elsie fell pregnant, with Mum, by an American soldier. By the time Mum was 8 months old, and before Elsie's husband returned home from the war, Mum had been adopted by her biological aunt.

Elsie used to occasionally visit Mum when she was young, under the guise of 'Queenie'. But the visits dried up and Mum would eventually lose touch with everyone who she considered to be her family.

Thanks to public records now being available online, we recently traced Mum's older half-sister, Pat. She still lived in Ipswich, where she had been born and once lived with Elsie. Elsie had long since died, but Pat had a whole family who we would meet and form a treasured relationship with.

In 2016, I drove Mum to Ipswich to meet Pat for the first time. It was an emotional union. I think for Mum this was the first time in her life that she was coming face to face with someone who felt like family, other than her own children. Mum and Pat chatted for hours, laughed together, and shared many tales of their own lives. Pat helped to fill in the gaps that Mum had about her early years.

Tragically, soon after their first meeting, Pat died. Mum lost the sister, and belonging, she had only just discovered.

But still, Mum's decision to leave me in Kent for two months at the age of 7 is one I will never understand, although I'm sure there was good reason. Sadly though, at that young age, I wasn't aware of the reason, only my own feelings.

After two months, Tina came to pick me up, or so I remember. And why didn't I stay with my dad, who lived locally? Why did I live with his sister? Did he not want me? I've never asked anyone these questions, choosing instead to protect them from the awkwardness. In hindsight, that means I've never given anyone the chance to answer them.

After a couple of months, I joined my mum and Tina in Essex. Originally, we moved from Kent to Hoddesdon, then to Broxbourne, and soon after to Nazeing where Mum bought our house, a traditional three-bed semi opposite my new school, on Hyde Mead.

Fearing the worst

Around this time, in the late 80s, Dad met Jan, who would go on to be my step-mum.

I remember staying at their house in Kent, around the age of 12, and sleeping in my older step-sister's bedroom, which was decorated with posters of her favourite rock bands. This particular night, I woke up and I had wet the bed. I poured lemonade over the sheets as a cover up.

I just remember feeling grateful that I didn't have my period – they had started a couple of months before. When they began, I felt so ashamed and dirty that I hid all evidence from Mum and Tina, and my friends. I didn't use sanitary products. I thought about stealing some from the bathroom cupboards but didn't want to raise suspicion, so instead I used folded sheets of toilet paper stuffed in my underwear.

I was terrified of everything. My existence felt vulnerable and fragile, even then. For years, into my teens, on windy nights, I would drag my duvet and sleep on the floor next to Mum's bed, to shield myself from the glass if the wind blew the windows in. I'd rather have slept on the carpet, cold but with someone, than alone with my fear.

At night, with the curtains open, I was scared to open my eyes for fear of seeing nuclear bomb clouds in the sky. With the curtains closed, my mind just convinced me the nuclear clouds were the other side of the window dressings.

Around the age of puberty, the recurring dreams I had had since I was 6 or 7 were analysed as being anxiety related. Those nightmares of having to squeeze huge foam shapes into small metal tubes used to paralyse me, night after night. I would lay in some strange state between being asleep and awake, where I would feel my existence yet not be able to move any part of my body.

One day, in the early 90s, it must have been 1991 or 1992 as I think I had just started secondary school, my eldest sister Angela had stayed the night. She slept in my bed so I got to sleep on the floor next to Mum's bed for the whole night – my favourite place to sleep. We woke in a panic the next morning and discovered we had been burgled. A cleaning company Mum used at the garage had secretly cut keys to our house, let themselves in during the night, and stole Mum's handbag with the keys for her petrol station and safe. Unknowingly, while we all slept, they let themselves into the petrol station and emptied the safe.

This version of the story – the truth – wasn't discovered until later the next night, after Mum and Tina had been accused and arrested for making a false claim. Mum was pinned to her wardrobe by the investigating police officers, told to confess, and taunted with the vibrators the police had found in Mum's wardrobe (which, so I overheard, were bought for her as a joke at an Ann Summers party).

Mum and Tina were locked in police cells at Harlow Police Station. Mum told of how she soon began to think she was guilty, and was close to confessing, when she caught sight of the cleaners being locked in cells between her and her daughter. This was all before CCTV was commonplace. Thankfully, the cleaners were caught on a single camera leaving the scene and there was enough evidence, including Mum's recovered handbag and the contents of the safe, to charge the two men.

Troubled teen

In 1992, Britain was in recession. Mum had worked hard to pay off most of her mortgage but, feeling the pinch of increased commercial rent and climbing interest rates, she struggled to make ends meet. Our home was repossessed.

Mum was stubborn and fiercely independent, never accepting any child maintenance from Roger or my dad, choosing to bring us all up unsupported.

One afternoon, I opened Mum's bedroom door and saw her sitting on her bed, sobbing and rocking back and forth. She was having a breakdown. I felt so helpless, like I was making things worse by being there; a burden.

School was never my favourite place. Not good, not bad, just average.

My friendships felt fake. I always wanted to be more popular, to fit in, like most kids I suppose.

I was clever but didn't want to show it, desperately wanting to be one of the cool kids, not one of the geeks. I was invited to join the extra studies group for academically gifted children but I felt like a fraud being there.

Life was a constant battle between fitting in, keeping under the radar, and being noticed. I craved attention but didn't want it when I had it.

Sitting in a maths lesson, I started to pull out my eyelashes. It's still something I battle with. I find it a comfort and never thought much of it, until I heard recently that it's a form of OCD called trichotillomania.

At home, alone in my bedroom, I started to cut myself on my ankles with a compass, under my socks so no one could see, feeling a sense of relief as the layers of skin split apart.

There is little to report of the next couple of years.

I don't have many memories of those times, good or bad, just a series of poor choice boyfriends and irresponsible decisions made with friends. Although I do remember spending a lot of time in my room, with my cat Tigger, longing to stop feeling lonely and misunderstood.

Tigger was a huge, angry, tabby cat who was the target of most of our neighbours. I spent countless nights with Tigger in my bed, stroking him till the early hours so that he didn't leave. I was even needy with him – a cat.

First love

I breezed through my exams with not much effort and no revision, leaving school with nine grade A-Cs. Only now can I appreciate how frustrating this must have been for my parents, knowing what I could have achieved if I had tried, instead of doing just the minimum I needed to get by.

At sixteen, I met my first love – Dean. We met on a night out, the day I collected my GCSE results. By this time Mum and I had moved to a rented flat in Harlow, after the repossession. Tina was nearby in a flat of her own. Angela lived in Bristol and Mark lived in Sussex.

As the months and years passed, Dean, his parents and sister became my family and I loved them all dearly. I told myself I felt safe, stable and cared for in their home. But how could I have done when the insecurity was within me?

Dean was a year older than me and worked as an estate agent when we met. I spent my summer holidays driving from appointment to appointment with him in his car. He'd park up around the corner from the property he was showing, and I'd sit and wait for him to finish. We spent every evening together. We were inseparable.

It was an incredibly serious relationship for a 16 and 17-year-old. We were a proper couple, attending weddings and events together. Dean took me on my first holiday at the age of 17, for two weeks in Ibiza. I spent Christmases with him and his family. I spent most of my time at his house, practically living there.

It was while I was alone at their house one day I started to binge on food from their cupboards and make myself sick. I first became bulimic at 16. It's so hard to say or even type those words. Even now, I have no idea why the bulimia developed at that time in my life, but it would stick around, unwelcome, for many years to come.

Another lost love

Dean met someone else after three years of he and I being together, and I can still remember the heartbreak. I had spent three years thinking of no other future than one with Dean and his family. In hindsight, it was an unhealthily serious relationship for someone to have at such a young age. My deep-rooted need to attach masked any problems we had in our relationship. I would have turned a blind eye to it all and stayed with him if he had wanted me.

Not only had I lost my first love, I'd lost his family unit. I felt left with nothing but the safety blanket of my eating disorder.

I went off the rails for a few months and caused my mum lots of upset. Coming home in the early hours, sometimes the next day, after long nights experimenting with drugs.

By the age of 19 I had taken speed, ecstasy and cocaine. I had abusive relationships, including being pushed head to toe into a bush of stinging nettles. The more toxic and controlling someone's behaviour, the more I felt loved by it. I had no self-worth and placed no value on my life.

I came very close to leaving out the previous section. I typed and deleted over and over. But if I'm to lay bare my honest account, then I need to share my whole truth – no more secrets – in order to free myself of the damaging shame and blame I've carried around for close to forty years.

At this time in my life, I felt constant anger and emotional turbulence. I have no idea why I hated myself so much. Looking back, I was crying out for love, for validation, for stability, and for a sense of belonging.

I knew I was causing my mum so much suffering, but I couldn't see any way to get on track. Pleading with Mum, I tried to explain I was being misunderstood. I had no idea how to articulate how I felt, or what I needed, but I knew I wasn't a bad person.

Mum called my dad one day in absolute despair. I'm not sure how that conversation went, what they discussed, or what they agreed. But Dad didn't come.

I like to think Mum didn't ask him to, otherwise I'm sure he would have been there at the drop of a hat. I knew I was causing Mum so much pain.

Despite only being 18, I decided to rent a room in a house owned by one of Dean's friends, Alex (name changed to protect his identity). I had only been there for two weeks, two very unsettled weeks, when some mutual friends, and friends of mine, came back to the house after a night out. The next morning, when everyone had gone home, some of Alex's possessions had been stolen, including a pair of designer jeans. I was embarrassed and couldn't face the responsibility or sleep there another night. Deep down I knew I should never have left home.

I asked Mum to take me back, which thankfully she did. Before I had a chance to go and collect my stuff, Alex had taken everything I owned to the dump. All I had were the clothes on my back and a carrier bag of essentials. I lost everything: clothes, photographs, memories, the christening bracelets I'd had since I was a baby. Even the Culture Club record I'd had since my third birthday.

Soon after I moved back home, my mum was to go on holiday with Angela, Tina, my brother-in-law Steve, and my nephew, Olly, to Majorca. I wasn't invited and I certainly wasn't welcome.

My mum needed this holiday; she needed the break from me. I knew I wasn't a bad person but I often felt like one. I remember kneeling in front of my mum as she sat on the sofa a few days before her holiday. I was sobbing and begging her to let me come too. I promised to be well-behaved, to be nice, to be calm. I longed to just lay on a sunbed and escape everything. But Mum stood her ground. She needed to escape me.

So, it was just me. With my thoughts and questions. *Who really understood me? Who loved me? Who was there for me?*

Around this time, in May 1999, I met Tom.

Finding my fairy tale

Despite the turbulence, I was studying fashion with marketing, part-time at Hertford College, and working a couple of days a week at a local petrol station, which Mum had introduced me to. I worked with a great bunch of girls and we had so much fun.

I had spotted a boy who came in regularly in a company van branded 'CF Oakes' – a local firm of bathroom and kitchen fitters. They had a fuel account at the petrol station so most days one of the team would come in to fill up with diesel. Every time a van pulled in, I would look to see if this handsome, blonde boy was behind the wheel. When he was, my tummy would do flips. He made me so nervous.

The girls knew he had caught my eye and they would always force me to serve him, which should have been exciting, but nerves made it so awkward and we never spoke or so much as made eye contact. To me, he was so beautiful. He looked like Leonardo DiCaprio in 'Titanic'.

One afternoon, I was working with a friend of Mum's called Pat. Pat was so full of life, always laughing and joking with the regulars.

In came Ian, a member of the CF Oakes team, on foot, as their office was only a short walk away from the petrol station. The usual jokes and banter were in full flow and Pat let Ian know that I had my eye on the young and handsome member of the team! I blush just retelling the tale. Ian hinted the feelings were mutual. The embarrassment turned to excitement. What could be more thrilling for a just turned 19-year-old than the guy she had been admiring from afar might just have been admiring her too?

One Monday morning, a few weeks later, in pulled a CF Oakes van with the handsome boy behind the wheel. I was working with Pat again, who was squealing with excitement and making me feel sick to the stomach! I had been replenishing the papers in the rack outside the shop and insisted to Pat that she HAD to serve him. I felt so painfully awkward. Terrified, I hid out the back of the shop until he had been and gone.

Or so I thought.

Without me realising, he had walked back in as I headed outside, and we came face to face in the doorway of the shop.

'I think I saw you on Saturday night at the country club,' I said nervously. It was the first thing I could think to say.

'I wasn't there, it must have been some other good-looking geezer,' was his ice-breaking first line. Then came the words that I had been longing for: 'If I give you my number will you come out for a drink?'

'Of course!' I answered. I had no doubt in my mind. We took some till roll from the counter and he wrote down his number. I still have that treasured piece of paper.

But I didn't call. I lost count of the number of times I picked up the phone. This was before most people of our age had mobile phones. Tom had given me a landline number for his parents' house. What if his mum or dad answered? What if it was awkward? What if we had nothing to talk about? Safer not to call, I decided.

The next day, the Tuesday evening, I was back at work. The news had spread and the girls knew what had happened the morning before. There was a phone call for me so I headed into the office. It was Tom. The girl I had been working with that evening knew I was too shy to call. Without me knowing, she had phoned Tom's home. We spoke for an hour. It was incredible. He was so confident and made me laugh so much. I knew even then something special was about to happen.

The next day we arranged to go on our first date. It was the 26 May 1999, a hot spring day. The day Manchester United went on to win the Champions League Final (before going on to win the treble).

Tom picked me up from home in his K reg, immaculate, dark blue BMW 3 Series. It had a light grey leather interior which was so over polished I slid in the front seat as soon as my clothes touched the edge of it.

We headed to what was then 'City Limits' restaurant, between Epping and Loughton. The Manchester United game was on TV and we sat and chatted over a few drinks. Tom came back from the bar but this time he sat next to me instead of opposite me and held my hand, pretending to look at my fresh nails as an excuse to do so. We kissed for the first time, rushed and nervously, if I remember.

We left the restaurant after a couple of hours. The sun was setting and we drove along the country roads with the windows down, listening to 'As' by George Michael and Mary J Blige blasting through the speakers. I had the biggest smile on my face.

Trying to hide my excitement, I leant my head back against the head rest and turned to the side, facing away from Tom. Happy tears welled in my eyes – was this the first page of my own fairytale?

Mum was in Bristol at the time. As it was Angela and Steve's wedding anniversary, she was babysitting Olly while they went away for a few days to celebrate. Tom and I arrived back at my flat. Trying to be a true gent, he walked me to the door. I had a free house so he came in. The first thing he saw on the side was a note from Tina saying: *Good luck with the Oakes boy!*

We sat in my room for a short time, listening to music and kissing on my bed, like two teenagers newly in love, before he left to go home.

One Sunday afternoon, less than two weeks after our first date, we drove to a park and laid on the grass looking up to the sky. It was a warm afternoon; the sun was shining. We both said the words 'I love you' for the first time. I knew then we would spend our lives together.

I felt such a pain in my heart as he dropped me off at work that afternoon and I sobbed as we cuddled and said goodbye. I remember considering leaving my job for good, just to delay that goodbye till the next day. I was infatuated with Tom and my happiness already relied deeply on him.

Fitting in

Tom's family welcomed me as their own from the first time I met them, just three days after our first date. Tom had taken me home to introduce me to his parents but, to my surprise, the whole street wandered in to meet who Tom had affectionately referred to as 'the petrol girl' before we began talking.

During the first three months of our relationship we saw each other every day. As I didn't drive, he would come to my flat or pick me up and take me to his parents' house. I loved nothing more than lying on the sofa with him, comforted, my head in his arms, watching films and eating pick and mix.

It's still one of my favourite things to do and where I feel most safe. Although it's something we need to make the time to do more often.

Tom is the oldest of four children: he has two brothers, Charlie and Sam, and a sister, Kate. When Tom and I met, Kate was 19, Charlie was 14, and Sam was 10.

Tom's parents, Jackie and Steve, had a huge circle of friends. Their home was always so full of people, noise, fun, playfighting and parties.

Kate, the only daughter, was away at university when Tom and I met but I had heard so much about her. Being a young girl with such insecurities, naturally I wondered if she would like me. Would her friends like me? In her eyes, would I be good enough for her big brother?

When I met Kate for the first time, she was so warm and welcoming. She was (and still is) so beautiful, so confident, the life and soul of every party. Did Tom want a girlfriend more like her?

I never felt good enough for Tom or his family and it took many years before I could be myself instead of the extroverted, fake person I thought they wanted me to be.

I always felt so much shame for hiding this story, especially in the early days of our relationship. His textbook childhood and upbringing were worlds apart from how I felt from such a young age.

Would he think I was insecure, needy?

In contrast, he was so confident, sociable, carefree, good-looking, charismatic...everything I felt I wasn't.

Mum and Tina moved to Bristol when I was nineteen. I remember the day Mum left. In the run up to it, I was so excited. My friend Maxine was moving in and we planned movie nights with the girls, and parties, and talked about ideas we had for decorating. But the morning Mum was leaving, I felt gutted, devastated. She packed up the last of her stuff and loaded the car. We hugged and both sobbed. I remember wondering if I could ask her to stay but I thought it was too late. She later told me she cried all the way to Bristol and approached every junction wondering whether to get off and turn back.

Moving to Bristol with them was never an option for me. I had Tom and wanted to stay with him. But I had to start taking some responsibility for my life.

Growing up

When Mum moved to Bristol and left our flat, Maxine moved in. I left college and started working in a data entry role for a company called Banktec, which processed credit card applications, so I could afford to pay rent and live independently. Whilst for many people data entry is a bore, I enjoyed the repetition, the silent working environment, and the daily challenge of who could key in and process the most applications in one day. Day in, day out, I was on the leaderboard and often at the top.

I've always been conscientious and hard-working. Mum and my siblings are the same. We were brought up with the belief that however small the job or task, we do it the best we can.

Work, during these years, was just about earning money to keep a roof over our heads and funding the weekends. Mondays were spent dissecting the weekend that had passed and Tuesdays to Fridays were spent planning the next. Occasionally, I took slimming tablets and amphetamines to work, in a quest to lose more weight by the next weekend.

In 2000, when I was 20, I took a job in the applications processing department of a local charity called Motability. Dad was registered disabled and had a Motability car. I felt close to him while I was at work. Within a year, I had moved to the fundraising department as a database administrator. This was my introduction to fundraising and what was the start of my career in the charity sector.

My insecurities soon began to surface in my relationship with Tom. I would set my alarm each morning for 07:00. If I didn't get up at 07:02 (on the dot), I told myself Tom would leave me for someone else. This went on for years.

Despite me abiding by the clock setting ritual with absolute precision, and many other traits of OCD, Tom and I, like any other teenagers in a relationship, had our ups and downs and we split up a couple of times. Never for longer than a day or two.

One Sunday afternoon, feeling sick with insecurity, I confronted Tom about why he had seemed a little distant. Looking back, I doubt he had, I expect it was me being particularly needy. We both broke down and he said it wasn't working between the two of us. Not the reaction I expected. Why did I do this to myself? Why did I force him away?!

After arguments, tears, and reluctance from me, he took me home, back to my flat with Maxine. That night, after crying myself to sleep with heartache, I had the same recurring anxiety dreams that I'd had as a child.

Tom and I exchanged a few texts during the next week. After an emotional reunion, we reconciled. I couldn't consider a future without him.

A couple of months passed, and the same thing happened. Riddled with insecurities and a failing, overwhelming need to control Tom, I admitted defeat. This time I left. The intensity and the pain I was causing myself was too much.

Tom's dad, Steve, was celebrating his 50th birthday with a huge party. We went to the party together and I stayed at their house after.

The next day, while everyone was together, whilst Tom's dad was opening his presents and the house was full of celebration, I went home and asked not to see Tom again.

It had been my decision; I had taken control, albeit half-heartedly.

I went out that night with the girls and saw a guy I had noticed before. It was while I was talking with him that I began to wonder if Tom and I would be able to reconcile and move forward without the drama. I went home on my own and sobbed into Maxine's arms again. I had so much love to give but I just needed some in return. Why couldn't I keep one loving, stable relationship? Why did all these people I love, and who said they loved me, leave me?

The following few days were a bit of a blur. I expect my memory is a haze because, at the same time, my dad was having a double lung transplant and was in intensive care, in Harefield Hospital.

The following Friday night, Tom came to see me after work. It was during this conversation that he and I committed to each other, to a lifetime together. We reflected on how we had both grown up, matured and appreciated what we loved and needed in each other. I was 23 and Tom was 24. We met when we were too young, but we were ready to settle down together.

We moved in together in September 2003, bought our first house in January 2005, and got engaged in December of the same year.

A few weeks before his proposal, I confessed that I'd had bulimia since I was 16, but that I had recently stopped. I hadn't. I felt like I needed to open up, to share some of my truth so I could move on to our future.

I made an appointment with our GP who referred me for counselling. I met the counsellor once and we had no connection. I cringed talking to her and fed her countless lies that she couldn't see through. *Does she have no experience of eating disorders?* I thought. Surely, if I had referred myself, I needed some help and I wasn't as okay as I was making out. I never saw her again.

Wedding pressure

On the 26 May 2007, we had a big, white wedding surrounded by all our friends and family. Exactly eight years, to the day, after our first date.

My dad was fully recovered from his lung transplant and was able to give me away. He cried the whole day, including throughout his speech, but he was the proudest man to walk this earth. The big occasion wasn't his thing, but he stood tall, said his words, and made me the proudest daughter.

With the pressures I felt of a hen trip to Marbella, a wedding with all eyes on me, and our honeymoon to Barbados, my eating disorder was at its peak. I was flitting between restriction and bulimia from one day to the next; avoiding food if I could, binging and purging if I couldn't.

My wedding dress had to be taken in by two dress sizes as I had lost so much weight in the run up to the big day.

Our honeymoon was at the Fairmont Royal Pavilion on the west coast of Barbados. It was stunningly beautiful and it's a place I'd love to take our children one day. It's a place I need to revisit to correct the memories.

Despite some special memories of us swimming in the sea and watching movies in our room overlooking the ocean, I'm also reminded of the lies I told after every meal. I desperately needed to get rid of the food I had overeaten. I was close to the lowest weight I have ever been, but I still felt fat, ugly and not good enough, or worthy of having Tom by my side. *People must think he has married below his own standard* was the lie I told myself as I walked next to him.

Where do I belong?

My nephew, Samuel, was christened in Bristol soon after our wedding. After the church service we celebrated with a BBQ at Tina's house. Roger, her dad, was there. It was a lovely summer's day and we were all in the garden, chatting, eating and drinking.

Tom and I went inside to get another drink and as we returned to the garden my family had grouped together for a photo, without me.

In my mind they had conspired and waited for me to leave the garden before getting together. Whether this was the case or not (I'm sure it wasn't), deep down I had the sense that I didn't quite fit in.

Where did I belong?

I hadn't lived in Kent since I was 7. I had never lived at my dad's house, so that didn't feel like home. I didn't feel good enough for Tom and his family, so they didn't feel unconditional. I had never lived in Bristol, which was now home for my mum and sisters, so that didn't feel like home either.

Becoming (Mum)

I came off the contraceptive pill in the summer of 2008. Late in January 2009, it suddenly occurred to me I hadn't had a period for a couple of months. My periods hadn't quite settled down since coming off the pill but I took a pregnancy test anyway. Two positive tests left me in complete shock.

I drove to find Tom at work and burst into tears on the street outside the house he was working in. I felt complete and in love from the minute I saw those positive lines. I had an immediate, unconditional connection to the baby growing inside me. This love could never be broken. This unborn child would need me. I had my purpose.

I made myself sick two to three times a day from the ages of 16 to 32. I remember one of my lowest days. It was the day of my twenty week scan when I was pregnant with our son, Ted. I used to squeeze my fist in the gap between my rib cage and my bump to force myself to vomit. I was painfully concerned that I might be risking my pregnancy and our baby's health, but it wasn't enough to stop my eating disorder, the self-harm, the punishment I gave myself.

While pregnant with Ted I was diagnosed with gallstones. I was convinced it was caused by the abuse I had given my body for so long, but that didn't stop me from resorting back to the bulimia soon after giving birth.

Teddy eventually came into the world on 10 October 2009, two weeks after my due date, and after a thirty-three-hour labour. The most precious, little, red-haired baby I had ever laid eyes on. His first cry sounded like a little lamb. He was born in the early hours of Saturday morning and soon curled up peacefully on me, taking his first feed, for thirty cherished minutes.

Soon after, Tom cradled him in his arms, facing the window. I could see the tears pouring from Tom's eyes in the window's reflection. I know not every parent is blessed with that immediate, unconditional love but I'm so grateful that I was.

Dad and Jan made the journey from Kent to Cambridge that morning and dropped a card and a present off for us with the nursing staff, not wanting to disturb Teddy, Tom and I during our first precious hours alone together.

Later that afternoon, Tom's family drove to Addenbrooks Hospital to see us with a bottle of champagne for themselves, and a baguette and a tub of paté for me! We were the loudest on the ward, and we all celebrated together.

I was 15.10 stones when I went into labour with Ted. I know because I weighed myself every day during my pregnancy. I put on five stones in total. Post-pregnancy weight loss was an exciting project I dedicated my mind to. I created a spreadsheet which I filled in with absolute diligence and dedication every day. I wouldn't stop until I had lost six stones and got down to 9.10 stones, which I did, eventually.

At one point, my weight was stuck at just over ten stones so I resorted to regular colonic irrigation to shift the last few stubborn pounds, travelling from one clinic to the next so I could have more treatments than I was allowed.

We tried for a couple of years for another baby. Unsurprisingly, my body wasn't going to accommodate another pregnancy. My periods were all over the place.

When Ted was 2, I was admitted to hospital with kidney stones, which I had to have surgically removed and a stent fitted. What damage was I causing my body? I was still making myself sick, even in the hospital.

Soon after the surgery, I fell pregnant with our daughter, Kit. After having Kit, I lost most of my baby weight through meal replacement shakes, laxative teas and restriction. For some unknown reason I didn't have any urge to binge and purge. In fact, the thought terrified me. But, after having the contraceptive implant fitted, I lived in a constant state of PMT and my binge eating was at a peak. I put on three stones in six months and felt so emotional, turbulent and angry that I begged for the implant to be removed.

Life as a family of four was good. Like many families, we juggled work and childcare alongside family holidays and great times as the children grew from babies to toddlers.

My two babies are my everything, like they are for most parents. I would say I am overly protective of them, increasingly more so as they have got older. They are now 10 and 7 and I struggle leaving them with anyone, including family members or friends. I still want them to sleep in my bed. I don't want to miss a single school run. I want them to have what I felt I needed but didn't have when I was younger: a strong internal sense of belonging. Not loneliness.

Living grief

In 2017, my life was thrown into chaos, even by my own measures.

One Sunday, in late August, the day after arriving in Portugal, our favourite place where we spent most of our summer holidays, I had a call from Angela.

Mum had set off in her car, a little red Clio, to Cribbs Causeway shopping centre to buy birthday presents for Ted and our nephew, Matthew. On her way there, she had had a major stroke. She began to lose the feeling in the left side of her body. She had managed to pull over, phone Angela, explain what was happening and describe where she was.

Angela called 999 and within minutes an ambulance was on its way. In a strange coincidence, Angela's eldest son, Oliver, who had only recently passed his driving test, was nearby.

Olly managed to get to Mum before the ambulance and sat in the car with her. At the tender age of 18, I can't imagine how scary it must have been for Olly to watch his granny suffer a major stroke, or for Mum to feel it happen to her body and her brain whilst sitting in front of her oldest grandchild. Olly travelled in the ambulance with Mum to Southmead Hospital, where she would stay for five months.

Mum had had a brain hemorrhage caused by high blood pressure. She was critically unwell. I sat on the beach on the phone to my siblings, faced with the decision of leaving Mum to die within three days, or operate to drain the hemorrhage but risk causing irreversible brain damage.

I battled with the idea of travelling back to the UK, where I would have been helpless, or staying with my family in Portugal and letting them, at least, enjoy their holiday.

My best friend, Tasha, her husband, Jack, and their three young sons were away with us. I'll always be so grateful for having them there. While my thoughts were preoccupied with Mum, Tom, Tasha and Jack were able to entertain the kids and create special memories for them. I'm sure I wasn't the best company.

We were staying in Vale do Lobo, which is my favourite place. It feels like home, my tranquil place, my sanctuary. In fact, my life's dream is to have a home there one day where Tom, the kids and I can spend all the school holidays.

Jack had lost his dad, John, to cancer many years before, when we were all teenagers. Jack, by appearance, is a tough guy, a man's man. An ex-rugby player with a bald head and a fully-grown beard since the age of 15. Jack lost his dad when we were all too young and immature to give him the support he needed.

The day Mum was having her surgery, we were spending the day on the beach. I'd been waiting all day for the call to say she was going to theatre. I had knots in my stomach and constant nausea only, ironically, this time I didn't want to be sick.

We went to lunch in the beach bar and I barely touched my food. We sat with our feet in the sand watching the kids playing and digging, and splashing in the sea. We drank mojitos, strawberry daquiris and bottles of Whispering Angel like the world would soon be in short supply. Laughter turned to tears and back again to laughter.

Jack and I spoke about our parents. Jack spoke openly about this loss and his grief and I believed

I was starting the same journey. I started to grieve the Mum I would lose.

Mum had lived on her own since she divorced Dad thirty years before. She was fiercely independent and wouldn't want to exist in a care home, being fed through a tube, unable to communicate, which was the prognosis we were given. If my sisters and my brother had made the decision to let Mum go, I would have agreed. But they didn't. They wanted to give her a chance to live. The operation went ahead and seemed to be a success. But Mum wasn't through the worst.

Over the course of the next seven weeks, Mum went on to overcome many setbacks. On at least two occasions we were told she wouldn't make it through the night.

One weekend in early September, I spent the weekend in Bristol. I hadn't been there during the previous few days as Kit had started school and was extremely unsettled. She needed me too. I needed to be there for her, at least in body. I wasn't always there in mind. I travelled back home from Bristol to Essex on the Sunday evening, back for Kit returning to reception on the Monday.

That Monday evening, I was at football training with Ted when Angela called to say Mum had sepsis and it wasn't looking good. Mum was going to die but they would try to keep her alive until I got there. Mark couldn't drive to Bristol from Brighton as he'd had a few glasses of (medicinal!) red wine. As an inspector for Sussex Police, there was no way he was risking driving over the limit. Mark poured another glass and toasted his goodbye to Mum; something she would have approved of.

I jumped in the car with a carrier bag containing a pair of knickers and a toothbrush, and began the one hundred and sixty mile journey to Bristol. It was dark and pouring with rain.

Angela called twice, whispering next to Mum, to see how long I would be. It was on this journey I had my first panic attack. I couldn't feel my legs or my arms and my heart was beating out of my chest.

For anyone who doesn't know the route from Essex to Bristol, it's motorway the whole way. Two of the worst motorways (if there is such a thing as a good one): the M25 and the M4. *Do I drive fast, too fast, to get there in time to say my goodbye to Mum, or do I drive sensibly and get there in one piece?*

I called Dad. Without even posing the question, he told me: 'Keep safe, take it easy, don't drive too fast and stop if you need to.'

I took his advice and put Ed Sheeran's '÷' album on shuffle. Poignantly, the first song to come on was one I hadn't heard – 'Supermarket Flowers'. In case you're not familiar with the song or its lyrics, here they are:

I took the supermarket flowers from the windowsill
I threw the day-old tea from the cup
Packed up the photo album Matthew had made
Memories of a life that's been loved
Took the 'Get Well Soon' cards and stuffed animals
Poured the old ginger beer down the sink
Dad always told me, 'Don't you cry when you're down'
But, Mum, there's a tear every time that I blink
Oh, I'm in pieces. It's tearing me up but I know
A heart that's broke is a heart that's been loved
So, I'll sing Hallelujah
You were an angel in the shape of my mum
When I fell down you'd be there holding me up
Spread your wings as you go
And when God takes you back
He'll say, 'Hallelujah, you're home'
I fluffed the pillows, made the beds, stacked the chairs up
Folded your nightgowns neatly in a case
John said he'd drive, then put his hand on my cheek

And wiped a tear from the side of my face
And I hope that I see the world as you did 'cause
I know
A life with love is a life that's been lived
So, I'll sing Hallelujah
You were an angel in the shape of my mum
When I fell down you'd be there holding me up
Spread your wings as you go, when God takes
you back
He'll say, 'Hallelujah, you're home'
Hallelujah
You were an angel in the shape of my mum
You got to see the person I have become
Spread your wings and I know
That when God took you back, he said,
'Hallelujah, you're home'

I felt my heart break.

A voice inside me asked, *Do you want to end it? Do you want to swerve into the central reservation and end this pain?* I answered with a half-hearted 'no' but it made me wonder who those two parts of me were – the person asking if I want to die and the person replying.

Somehow, despite the panic attack, the suicide consideration, the tears, the torrential rain and the heartbreaking music, I made it to Southmead Hospital.

I walked on to the ward, thinking I would be walking out without a mum.

I met Angela and Tina at Mum's bedside. They both looked as white as a sheet. Mum looked peaceful, like she was taking her last breaths. By this time, it must have been 22:00. The nurses explained they had given her some medication to control the pain – a last dose of chemotherapy grade antibiotic – so she was comfortable. Her 'obs' hadn't changed much in the last few hours so at 23:00 they told us to go back home, try to grab some sleep and that she would likely slip away in the morning. They would call us if anything changed in the night.

Angela went back to her own house nearby and I went to Tina's. We sat on Tina's sofa feeling quite numb. We spoke about music we'd play and people we needed to remember to invite to the funeral.

Mum's empty house was next door to Tina's, but I was too scared to sleep in there on my own. My nephew, Samuel, and my niece, Samantha, were fast asleep upstairs. I laid on the sofa and attempted to get some sleep. I lay in fear that Mum had died without us knowing and the first place her spirit would come was home. I laid under a blanket too scared to open my eyes in case I saw Mum's ghost.

The hospital didn't call. Tina and I drove back to Southmead to meet Angela at 09:00 as agreed.

By this point, every time I walked into the hospital I had to go straight to the toilet. The anxiety was causing my bowels to open without much warning. No time more than now, when I was hours, maybe minutes away, from saying goodbye to Mum. Watching her take her last breath. How would it be? Would I stop crying? Would the three of us scream and wail over Mum's body?

I met Angela and Tina at Mum's bed and the three of us were told the news…Mum had fought off sepsis. Not only had she fought off sepsis, she had fought off the worst case of sepsis the medical team had ever seen anyone fight off.

Mum went on to fight off pneumonia, collapsed lungs and delirium, as well as many other infections. She had an open drain in her brain, taking away the excess fluid. She couldn't talk and was confined to her bed, being fed through a tube, and she had a catheter.

Within a few weeks she was stable, but she was just a body in a bed.

On the 12 October 2017 we agreed to meet Mum's consultant as her slow progress had halted. We were all expecting to be told painful news.

I arrived at Southmead ahead of my sisters as the meeting was planned for 14:30 and I had left Essex straight after the morning school run.

As I walked in, Mum was awake. She said, 'Oh, hello,' completely out of the blue. The first words she had spoken in almost two months.

'Mum, you're talking,' I forced out, almost speechless, in complete shock.

'I feel like me again, I think I'm back,' were the next words I heard, and words I never expected. I was almost floored. The next sentence did knock me off my feet...'Let's not waste any more time being sad.'

I'm not sure whether Mum felt or knew the depth of those words. Deep down, I think she did. To me, those few seconds reversed years of pain, regret, upset and bad feeling. We both sobbed. I sat next to her hospital bed and sobbed in her arms. Despite Mum's vulnerability, fragility, and poor health, she was my mum and still felt like my protector.

She had to learn to eat, drink and talk again. She had been left paralysed but could go home, next door to Tina, but would need carers to visit four times a day.

We were told it was Mum's stubbornness which had kept her alive. Her refusal to give up, to die.

Mum's return home had been planned for weeks. She was apprehensive; we all were. Concerned for the pressure it would put on Tina next door and aware of the adaptations we'd have to make to Mum's home, and to all our lives.

Eventually, Mum's return home was finalised for the 25 January 2018.

The day before Mum returned home from hospital, my dad died.

My dad, my hero

Dad had been unwell since he was born prematurely with a hole in his heart. As an adult, he was diagnosed with a hereditary condition called Alpha-1 antitrypsin deficiency. AATD is a rare, inherited condition, which can cause lung and liver problems. It's thought that about twenty-five thousand people in the UK have the genetic condition, though most remain healthy so few have been diagnosed.

Dad wasn't so lucky. His life had been limited by the condition from a young age and he was on the transplant register by the time he was 41. He was confined to his house, eventually to a chair, and was on a constant supply of oxygen built into his home.

One night, in February 2002, at the tender age of 44, he had a call to say there was an organ match.

He was driven by ambulance from his home in Kent, to Harefield Hospital in Middlesex, to face eleven hours in theatre for a double lung transplant.

Dad hadn't laid flat for months, maybe a year or more, before his surgery. His lungs were too small and shrivelled, like prunes, for him to take in enough oxygen when laid down.

As I walked into intensive care to see him post-surgery, he was surrounded by wires in what seemed like a tiny bed in a huge room and he was lying down.

My step-mum, Jan (who I have dedicated a whole section to later in this book), was wetting his mouth with a swab-stick while he slept soundly. He was so calm, still, peaceful. A long way from the jerky, erratic breathing he had endured for years.

Jan and I sat either side of Dad's bed, holding his hands and looking at the miracle in front of us. Slowly, gradually, he opened his eyes. He looked at us and smiled. We watched as tears rolled down the side of his vulnerable, soft face.

Despite the lump in my throat, I held back the tears until I was in the hospital corridor. Once there, away from Dad's view, the tears poured. Jan held me in her arms and begged me not to cry.

She was holding her strength together and seeing me break down made her feel some weakness that she didn't want to let in.

Harefield saved Dad's life and changed mine. They gave me the years I needed with my childhood hero. The years I cherish. The years I will always appreciate. They gave Dad the precious time to be a wonderful grandparent and me the chance to witness it.

Dad made a quick recovery from his transplant and was soon home. We joked that he recovered quicker than David Beckham did from a broken metatarsal. I'll never forget the day he called me to say he had arrived home. I didn't believe it was him. His voice sounded so high pitched. He could finally breathe.

He survived sixteen years with his new lungs. Throughout those sixteen years he fought off a few infections, some of which were severe and required lengthy stays in hospital. Still, he never moaned. He was so thankful for every single second, each one a gift. He loved the simple things in life and had no time for nonsense, material things or anything that distracted him from his family.

His happy place was sitting on the beach enjoying some chips and an ice cream with Jan. His beloved sport was fishing. He also enjoyed time in the recovery yard with his brother, Mick, and spending time with Tom, the kids and me – his daughter who I know he treasured more than anything.

My step-brother, Pete, Jan's son, lives in Norfolk and Dad and Jan would spend their holidays there. Dad loved walking along the coastline in Bacton. Whatever the weather, he appreciated the view, the fresh air, the water, and being surrounded by the simple beauty nature offers.

Less than four months before Dad died, we spent a weekend in Bacton celebrating his 60th birthday. The kids gave Dad a Chelsea FC shirt with *Grandad* and *60* on the back. Little did we know at the time, he would soon be wearing the shirt in his final resting place.

I thought long and hard about whether to keep the shirt for the kids as a memory of their grandad, but I made the decision that it was a special gift for Dad, and I wanted it to stay with him. We had his love and his memories.

I will always be indebted to the person who lost their life to give Dad his. The donor whose lungs Dad meticulously cared for and appreciated until his last day.

We were able to create the most incredible memories.

In the years before he died, the impact of the high doses of medication began to take its toll on his kidneys and they soon began to fail. It was a slow deterioration and he never admitted he was becoming more unwell. 'It will be alright,' he'd always say.

He spent a long period in hospital soon after his 60th birthday. His kidney function was decreasing, he had no appetite so was losing weight, and he looked frail. He was allowed home for Christmas but was back in within days of the new year. His kidneys had failed, and he was put on dialysis. Gruelling dialysis. Night after night, lasting most of the night. He wasn't sleeping in the day and was gradually getting weaker.

Kit turned five on 9 January 2018. The kids and I went into Harefield the following day to take Dad some cake and to have a little party with him. I often study the photos from that evening. I look at Ted and Kit's faces and think we had no idea at the time they would soon lose their grandad. I look at Dad's face and wonder if he knew then just how unwell he was. Did he know then he would only live for another fortnight? If he did, was he scared? Sad?

On 21 January 2018, Ted was due to play in a rugby match for Bishop's Stortford but it was called off because the pitch had frozen. I had planned to go to Harefield with just Kit. As Tom's and Ted's plans had changed, they asked to come with us to see Dad. I checked in with Dad to see if that was okay, wondering if it would be too much for him, but knowing without any doubt he'd want to see us all.

The four of us jumped in the car and made the journey to Harefield. We had great fun with Dad, like we always did. The kids climbed around the bed and ate all of Dad's untouched sweets and crisps. We laughed and joked too loudly for a hospital ward full of very sick patients. Dad's face and eyes were full of pride and love like they always were.

After a couple of hours, we started to make our way out of the hospital. Tom and the kids gave 'Grad' (their name for Grandad) a kiss and a hug and said their I love yous.

Dad and I were on our own. I sat on his bed and noticed his legs were so skinny you could hardly see them under the flat sheets. We hugged. Properly hugged. I touched his skin, smelt his neck and felt his hair. I meant every word when I said, 'I love you.' And I listened intently as he echoed the words.

I walked to the car, climbed in and said to Tom, 'That felt like goodbye.'

Later that afternoon, Tom's mum and dad invited the family round for a Sunday roast. The house was full of noise and laughter, but I had a sinking feeling of sadness.

Jan phoned the next day to let me know Dad was in pain. Despite everything he had been through, he had never been in pain. The doctors were trying to work out what was causing the intense agony in his stomach. Things were feeling quite different. I could hear the concern in Jan's voice. She and I talked regularly over the next twenty-four hours. Dad was mostly sleeping, and the team were trying to control his pain. He had a severe infection, this time in his gallbladder.

Early on the Wednesday morning, Jan called after meeting with Anna, who had been Dad's consultant since his transplant sixteen years before. Through her own tears, Anna had told Jan they were beginning palliative care for Dad. There was nothing more they could do for him. His kidneys had failed, he was full of infection and he had sepsis.

I took the kids to school and was at the hospital by 10:00. I remember thinking, *I've been here before.* Only three months earlier I had arrived at Southmead hospital to say goodbye to Mum. *Will there be another miracle? Can Dad fight off sepsis too?* I wondered.

I walked into Dad's room. He was drifting in and out of sleep. He slowly opened his eyes, saw me and said 'hello' in the brightest voice he could muster. This was to be his last word.

Dad took his last breath at 18:00, with his wife, mum and daughter by his bedside. The emotion was suffocating.

Jan and I spent a couple of hours with Dad's body soon after he died, pottering around in his room, packing away his belongings for treasured, safe keeping.

I walked Jan back to her room at the hospital, then set off on my drive home with a sense of emptiness. By this time it was 22:00 and I spent the whole journey wondering how to tell the children the news their beloved Grad had died.

Tom opened the door to me and I began to cry, wondering if I would ever stop.

Ted came wandering into our room the next morning, before school, and I broke the sad news to him. I can't remember what I said, I just remember his reply: 'Don't be sad, Mummy, it means Grandad will always be with us now.'

Kit chose to stay off school. Ted was going to stay off too, but by 09.15 he asked to go in. I realised that morning just how resilient children are.

The following morning, before heading to Harefield to visit Dad in the chapel of rest, and before going to Uxbridge to register his death, I drove the children to school, attempting to face some sort of reality. The first song to play on the radio was Culture Club's 'I'll Tumble for Ya'. I'm convinced it was a message for me from Dad, to reassure me he was, and is, still around.

My dad is my hero. I've lost count of the times I heard the words, 'He was such a kind man.' The most positive light. An optimist. An appreciation for simplicity. In his memory, I vowed to dedicate my energy to my healing, to finding my right path.

In the time soon after Dad dying, I wrote the words I wanted to say at his funeral, and I spoke to my granny to piece together the early years of Dad's life.

Dad's cremation was on 16 February 2018. Understandably, Mum couldn't come with me. We laid white roses on Dad's coffin and I laid a blue and pink rose with messages from Ted and Kit. Tears fell from my eyes as I read Ted's message to Grad:

Dear Grandad,
I hope you had the best life, you were such a nice man.
From Teddy

Jan, Granny and I walked behind Dad's coffin into the chapel filled with those who loved him. I read his eulogy with an overwhelming sense of pain and pride.

Although painful, it was such a love-filled day. Tina and Mark came with Tom and I to celebrate the life of my dad, the man who, despite only being a few years older than them, was once their step-dad.

Tom drove us home from Kent after the funeral and we headed to Steve and Jackie's house as they were looking after the kids. They had spent the afternoon and evening playing traditional board games and were deep into a tense game of Solitaire when we arrived. They beamed with delight as we walked through the door and jumped up to greet us. As I looked at their innocent little faces, filled with such love, my heart broke as I began to grieve the loss of their Grad.

That night they climbed in bed with Tom and I and we all slept side by side, four people in a double bed. I needed their closeness and felt so thankful I had them to partly fill the huge Dad-sized hole I had in my heart.

Later that month, we went to Bristol. It was the first time I had seen Mum since she returned home, and since Dad had died.

I sat on the floor in front of Mum's chair. She had limited movement but put one arm around me, the arm she could move, and consoled me as I sobbed. Through tears, she explained how I loved my dad so much, that she loved him too but she couldn't live with him, that he and I always had a special bond. I started to feel angry about him being taken from me but I needed to protect the memories I had of the special relationship with my dad, my hero.

Jan

Dad was good friends with Pete when he met Jan, Pete's mum. He went on to build a life with Jan. They married in 1987 and I was their bridesmaid. I fondly remember shopping with Jan for ballet shoes to wear to their wedding.

I don't remember ever thinking anything negative about Jan when I was a child, although I'm sure I didn't appreciate her like I would come to as an adult.

Jan tirelessly cared for Dad; beyond the level you could ever imagine, for two decades. Mum has commented regularly over the years that she could never have done what Jan did for him.

They did everything together. Everything. Jan would go fishing with Dad. Dad would go to supermarkets with Jan and wait in the car while she wandered the aisles. They would visit Granny every Thursday and go to boot fayres and auctions looking for hidden treasures. We often joked that Dad was like 'Del Boy' but he never wanted to be a millionaire, he just wanted to make a few quid to get by.

I owe so much to Jan, not just because of how she cared for Dad, but also for how she remained such a constant in my life. Even when I was a turbulent and difficult teenager, I never felt judged by Dad or Jan. Of course, it must have been more difficult for my mum to witness my behaviour day-to-day, but I'm sure there were days when Jan told Dad I was a nuisance step-daughter. However, I never felt like she didn't support me.

Jan and I became very close after Dad's transplant, increasingly so as his health deteriorated in more recent years, and even more so after he died. I feel so blessed that Tom I have Jan in our lives, and that Ted and Kit have Jan as their grandma.

Camping trip

In August 2018, Tom, Ted, Kit and I went camping in Norfolk with Tina, Ian, Samuel and Samantha. It was becoming quite a tradition. Our first camping holiday was in Cornwall the summer before, just a few weeks before Mum's stroke.

But this time it was different; better. We spent as many afternoons and evenings sitting outside around a barbeque, drinking cider and playing games as we did the year before. But this year I fell in love with being outside. The smell of cut grass, the morning dew, the cold dawn air, the animals in the fields, the sound of the waves and the feeling of sand crunching between my toes.

The feeling of grounding and being in the moment was something I was starting to understand and appreciate.

One evening, Tina and I sat on our camping chairs, wrapped in blankets sipping gin and tonics. The kids were playing games a few metres from us and Tom and Ian were sitting nearby, probably drinking beers and talking about rugby.

I quizzed Tina on when her, Mum and Angela had started to feel signs of the menopause. My periods, while regular, had shortened in length and would only last two days. They were so light on the second day I wouldn't even need to use a towel, and they were certainly not heavy enough to use a tampon. I had started to feel my body temperature rise a few days before my period and my breasts would often feel tender.

I joked how Tom and I were relying on the withdrawal method as contraception but that we'd become a bit careless, having an accident a few weeks before. I was too sensitive to the hormones in the pill and as I was convinced I was peri-menopausal we weren't too concerned about prevention.

Memories of Mykonos

In mid-September 2018, Tom and I went away to Mykonos for the weekend with twenty of our friends to celebrate our brother-in-law, Martin, and our friend, Ed, turning forty.

The day before we flew Tom and I shared our unexpected but exciting news with Ted and Kit – Mummy was pregnant! We'd found out a few weeks before, but it took a while for us to get over the shock! They were going to have a baby brother or sister! They were overjoyed. Ralphie or Wren were the names they chose, and they beamed with delight as they ran into school and told their friends the next morning.

While waiting at Heathrow Airport for our flight, I excitedly called Mum and Jan to share our news. Jan and I sobbed as we agreed it had been thanks to Dad that we would have the wonderful new addition to our family. I was convinced it was a boy. Ralphie-John had a nice ring to it.

We arrived in Mykonos late afternoon on the Friday and all headed out for a gorgeous meal in the stunning bay, just a few minutes' walk from our hotel.

The following morning, we went on our tour of the island in a convoy of quad bikes; a chance to explore and take in the beauty of Mykonos. We headed to Scorpios for a drink before our cars took us Nammos Beach Club for the afternoon and evening.

Everyone was enjoying drinking champagne and cocktails, dancing on the tables and on the beach, and swimming in the sea. It was such a special time with a wonderful group of friends.

Often, I would place a hand on my tummy, so excited to be bringing our little baby into such a beautiful world. I didn't miss drinking; in fact, I liked having an excuse not to. I loved feeling so fresh and healthy, together – me and our unborn baby.

Two days later, sitting on the beautiful beach at Kalou Beach Club, with Tom's sister Kate, I said, 'Isn't it funny, even when you're pregnant with your third you still go to the toilet and worry you'll see blood?'

An hour or so later, I went to the toilet and my biggest fear had come true. Despite the high Aegean temperature, I felt myself go as cold as the ice in my mocktails.

I returned to our group and the colour drained from Tom's face as I told him. Our friends were so supportive as I burst into inconsolable tears and told them what had happened.

Tom and I took a taxi back to the hotel, where we stayed for the rest of the day and night. We felt so lonely and far from home; vulnerable, too far from the hospital, physically and emotionally miles apart from Ted and Kit.

The next day we flew back to Heathrow and I could think of nothing else but the physical and emotional emptiness inside me. I knew in my heart that it wasn't just a bit of spotting. I knew I had miscarried. My breasts no longer felt tender. I didn't feel pregnant anymore.

As soon as we walked into our home the kids ran to the door and their little faces looked so bright. Ted kissed my tummy and I knew I would have to plant the seed that everything might not be okay.

Introducing the concept of miscarriage to an 8-year-old boy is challenging at best, heartbreaking at worst. I explained that Mummy had had some tummy aches and would need to go to the hospital the next morning to check if everything was okay.

'Do you think everything is okay?' he asked wishfully.

'I really hope it is, darling, but I don't think so.'

I took the kids to school the next morning and Tasha called after she had done the same. 'I'm coming to the hospital with you,' she insisted. I thought I would have been fine on my own, but I am so thankful she knew what I needed even more than I did.

The Early Pregnancy Unit confirmed our worst fear: my hormone levels had dropped and I was no longer pregnant. Immediately my thoughts turned to Ted; he would be devastated. Kit was too young to really understand and, looking back, I was more concerned for Ted than I was even for Tom or myself.

Tom wasn't happy when I found out I was pregnant but he had come around to the idea. In Mykonos, he was so proud and delighted we would soon be adding another member to our family.

I headed straight to school at 15:00, twenty minutes before the school day would usually finish. If I had collected Ted at the usual pick up time, he would have asked me in the playground if everything was okay with the baby. I couldn't do that to him, or to me.

The office called down to Ted's class and he came to the school reception to meet me. 'Is everything okay?' he asked as he poked his head round the door. All I could muster was a shake of my head.

He fell to the floor in tears, with his head in his hands. I scooped him up like he was a newborn, held him and sobbed into the back of his head with his headmaster, Mr Watts, watching on, compassionately.

Breaking that news to Ted and Kit, but especially Ted, is still the most painful moment of my life.

Table for four

That night the four of us went to a local pizzeria. Trying to stay bright and positive for the children, I put on a smile and appreciated everything I had, instead of focusing on the baby that wasn't to be.

We ordered our food and sat with our drinks and the music playing. Tom burst into tears at the table, his eyes showing such loss and sadness. He took himself outside so the kids wouldn't see him cry.

Two or three times he came back to the table and had to walk away again. For him too, I wonder if the faces of our two babies made him wonder what the face of another baby might have looked like.

Instinctively, I focused my love and attention on Tom, Ted and Kit, on their loss, their grief.

I showered them with words of gratitude, appreciation for what we had, but never really showed any kindness to my own emotions.

Feeling vulnerable

Soon, everything began to feel unsafe, so vulnerable. I was terrified our children were going to die, get hit by a car, be shot while at school, develop a brain tumour. You name it, it crossed my mind.

I checked the boundary of the school to reassure myself no one could get in. Over and over, my mind played videos of a gunman entering their classes and all I could feel inside was the fear they would experience, and all I could see was the terror they would have on their faces.

On the short walk to school, I would insist they walked on the side away from the road. My heart would be in my mouth the whole journey as I dreaded a car mounting the curb and robbing them off their lives, robbing me of them.

I would place my hands on their chests as they slept and plead that their bodies be healthy inside. Behind their innocent white and pure skin, I was convinced there were tumours, unhealthy cells, poison that would take them away from us.

A few weeks before Christmas, I had my morning tea, opened the kids' vitamin boxes and noticed Ted had more left than Kit. *He's going to get a cold. He's going to be in hospital for Christmas. What if he has pneumonia? I bet he has an infection that will lead to sepsis!* The voice inside my head was on overdrive, relentless.

You know that feeling of fright as your foot slips on the stairs? That is how I felt during every waking second.

I couldn't cope like this for much longer. My heart palpitations were constant. It would take me hours to fall asleep, only to wake up an hour later and lay restless for another three to four hours. My walls were caving in, the ceiling was crushing down and I had no mind space remaining. The box I was living in was becoming smaller and smaller, with less air and little light.

'Social anxiety' was a term I discovered and immediately related to. I would look forward to an event or night out in the weeks and months before, yet as the day drew closer I would dread seeing people.

Will I feel awkward? Will I have anything to say to people? Will anyone make me dance? I don't want to dance! Who will babysit? Will the kids cope without me? Will they feel unsafe, lonely or scared? My constant, internal chat was exhausting.

Because of this, I missed out on so much. I let down so many people I love. One of my motivations for writing this book was to offer some understanding to the people I disappointed.

Tom always made excuses for me and represented us on so many occasions: the christening of our friend's children, a weekend in Ibiza with my best friends to celebrate my childhood friend's 40th birthday, many nights out, birthday parties, weddings… The list of excuses became so long that I felt embarrassed to send Tom off to yet another event without me.

I knew I was letting people down, that people could see through the lies, but in my mind that was better than being there, often away from the kids, and feeling so uncomfortable.

It had been building for some time, this physical and emotional sense of tension inside me. My heart was racing, my mind felt full to the brim, and my stomach was constantly in knots.

I woke up one morning and the feelings were so intense, my mind was so full, I couldn't think how to get Ted and Kit up, dressed and ready for school. I held the sides of my head, closed my eyes and just wanted to scream, cry, throw myself on the floor and beg for help.

I had hit rock bottom. I couldn't see that there was any way out.

Asking for help

Secretly, I made an appointment with my GP for that afternoon. I met with Doctor Taqhar and I was so grateful to see her face. The flood gates opened. I didn't need to hold in this pressure any longer.

I sobbed and sobbed to her and I felt such a sense of relief. I was diagnosed with depression and anxiety disorder, put on antidepressants (Sertraline), and referred for counselling.

On the way home from the surgery I called Tom and my in-laws to confess. I couldn't carry on how I was. Tom came home and sobbed with me.

In that very moment, the lowest of times, admitting 'defeat', being held whilst talking, I felt like I could already climb the first step back up.

Within a few days of my GP appointment, I received a call for an initial counselling assessment. After a ten to fifteen minute conversation, I was told I wasn't suicidal so wasn't a priority. Was I not even good enough at being mentally unwell?

The antidepressants made me feel worse for the first month. I had zero motivation and I couldn't concentrate on anything. Work, home, chores around the house...I just had no interest. I found it difficult to hold a conversation. I could hear what people were saying but I just couldn't think of anything to reply and, to be honest, I didn't really have any interest.

The medication had created some mind space, but the feeling of overwhelm had been replaced with a sense of nothingness. I also had no appetite. Extensive internet browsing had reassured me that these side effects were all quite normal.

After a month or so I started to feel better, back to myself, albeit a version of myself with very little emotion. The anxiety and panic had eased off but so had my feelings of happiness, love, pleasure and excitement. I can only describe it as shaving off each end of the emotional spectrum by 25%.

Eventually, two months later, I was offered an appointment for counselling. Nervously, I drove to the session, pulled up in the car park and received a call to say the therapist had double booked and I would need to reschedule for the following week. That day came and, for whatever reason, I didn't want to go. I made my excuse and cancelled the appointment.

I had to invest in myself. I had to pick myself back up.

This section of the book was meant to end here. But life had other plans.

The unexpected extra chapter

If the production of this book had gone according to plan, this chapter wouldn't be here. Instead, I'm adding it almost a year after the previous pages were written.

Over the last twelve months, before writing this chapter, I had been living and breathing the #FortyTools that follow. Living proof that they work. That day-to-day rituals, routines, techniques and tools can help preserve positive mental health and mindset.

But life threw a curve ball. Throughout the summer of 2020, most of which was spent in lockdown thanks to Coronavirus, Mum's health slowly deteriorated. She was admitted to Southmead hospital with breathing difficulties in May and, soon after, diagnosed with heart failure and low levels of oxygen and high levels of carbon dioxide in her blood. Lockdown made hospital visits a challenge for all of us, especially Mum. Eventually, after nights on carbon dioxide therapy and days on oxygen, she was allowed to go home.

With a newfound determination, Mum remained bright for a few weeks and began to get back some quality of life. Sadly, the optimism subsided as her oxygen levels gradually declined, and she was soon back in hospital. This continued throughout most of the summer, in and out of hospital. We were told more than once that it was 'touch and go'.

Angela, Mark, Tina and I lived with a knot in our stomachs, the familiar feeling of anxiety that had not long departed. But Mum remained as brave and determined as ever.

Southmead Hospital opened its doors again to Mum in September. Her health had deteriorated enormously and we began to realise a return home, with any independence, was becoming less likely. She would need 24/7 care. We explored all options, including a care home, a hospice and a live-in carer. But nothing seemed quite right. Nothing felt right for mum, like home as she knew it.

We were told Mum had picked up an infection which, along with COPD, heart failure, respiratory failure and the physical effects of a stroke, meant little quality of life. As her children, we began to have conversations with Mum about her wishes. With a completely sound mind, she told us she had had enough. She felt it was her time to go. As hard as this was to hear, we agreed to respect her wishes.

It was Sunday night, on the 27 September, and Mum's consultant told us, and her, that on paper they should have been able to treat the infection but her body was giving up the fight. Bravely, Mum instructed the medical team to stop treatment. The medicine, masks, intervention, and week-long stays had become too much. And who could disagree with her?

I was with Mum at the time. Her consultant asked to talk to me outside the room, to ensure I, and Mum, knew what this would mean. Mum was likely to live for 'a high number of hours or a low number of days'. I can't remember how I felt. A mixture of relief, sadness, fear and anxiety, I suppose.

Mum had told us she didn't want to spend any time alone as she was frightened. Tina came back to the hospital and vowed to spend the night with Mum. A bed was set up alongside Mum's and the two of them kept each other company. Ted and Kit had school the next morning, so I set off from

Bristol at 22:00 to get them ready for the next day, before returning to Bristol straight after the school drop off.

It was Monday 28 September, which would have been Dad's birthday. Angela and Tina were with Mum when I arrived. The three of us sat around Mum's bed, laughing, joking, keeping Mum entertained and in good spirits. Although she mostly slept, she did wake up for her little pots of ice cream.

The palliative care team authorised Mum's wishes. She had only one: a gin and tonic. Our faces must have shown such mixed emotions. For anyone who has lived through these moments, you'll know there are still glimpses of happiness, even humour.

Mum seemed quite stable all day. Sleepy, but slightly alert when she was awake. Each time she woke up she looked around, surprised to still see us and the four walls of her hospital room. It took a few moments for her to realise where she was, and when she did she was either cross to still be alive or amused by her own thoughts. She hadn't quite yet made it to the white gates of Heaven, even joking that Dad wasn't letting her in, in case she ruined his birthday.

Later that evening, Samuel and Samantha came in to say their goodbyes. They were so brave. They had lived with their granny for most of their lives. My heart still aches for them and for how proud they both made us all that evening. I'm not sure I would have had their strength at 12 and 16.

As they were leaving, the nurse came in with Mum's favourite ice cream. 'I don't need it, it's too late, I'm going now,' are the words Mum spoke.

Tina went home for the night and it was my turn to have a sleep over with Mum. In the run up to these hours I had asked Angela, Mark and Tina whether they wanted to be with Mum at the end. Of course, we didn't know when that might be.

The final hours of Dad's life were beautiful, peaceful. Despite being ready to go, Mum was scared. She would grip our hands and tell us so. With the greatest determination, I knew Mum could have the same beautiful and peaceful end of life experience as Dad had had. I knew deep within my soul I could play a part in making that happen.

At around 19:00, I asked the nurses to get Mum ready for bed early. She had been late to bed the night before and spent the evening being quite unsettled. Before 'Emmerdale' had finished, Mum and I were both in our beds, the lights were off, and we watched Mum's soaps. She was mostly sleeping, but I knew she could hear them.

I moved between my bed and Mum's bedside throughout the night. We listened to sleep meditations for hours. The energy in the room was so calm, so still. Mum was settled. Around 02:30, I noticed Mum's breathing was slowing and her skin was cooling.

Just before 03:00, with my hand on her chest, she took her final breath. It was serene and everything we could have wished for, for our mum.

Tina came to the hospital and we sat next to Mum for a couple of hours, pottering around and gathering her belongings, saying our second-to-last goodbyes.

On the 23 October 2020, Mum made her final journey to Westerleigh Crematorium, in Bristol. I didn't have the strength for Mum's funeral as I found for Dad's. Perhaps it was the accumulation of saying goodbye to both parents.

Mum had the most beautiful wicker coffin but seeing it, so innocent and pure, was devastating for us all. The service was limited in number due to Covid restrictions but it did make the service intimate and personal. Perhaps this was why emotions were so raw; we didn't have to put on a brave face.

Tom and I sat either side of Ted and Kit on the cold wooden pew, with Mum's coffin in front of us, covered in a stunning display of white flowers. We sobbed in each other's arms as the words of 'Supermarket Flowers' played loudly and silenced the room.

I can't tell you what this journey through grief will be like. It's unpredictable. But I do know I have #FortyTools to get me through.

This book was, in the most part, written when my mum was alive. But it was finished after she died. I reflect on whether the words in the book were disrespectful of her as my mum. I really and truly hope that's not how it comes across. The pain and suffering I have felt for many years of my life is no fault of my parents or family.

When I knew Mum was nearing the end of her life, I found a bereavement counsellor, Jan, and asked her to help me through my grief. By chance, my first appointment with her was booked in for, what turned out to be, the day after Mum died. Within the first couple of hours of speaking with Jan she summed up the root cause of my anxiety and self-hurt: 'All your life you've felt like no one got you. You felt lonely, until you had your children. That's why your greatest fear in life is being apart from them and feeling lonely again'.

Just like that, I understood myself, for the first time.

Post-Traumatic Growth

Digging deep

I had to turn my life around, dig-deep and live my life, for I now realise how short and precious it is.

Slowly, intuitively, I've developed a tried and tested list of #FortyTools and techniques to show myself love. To create positive energy. I've noticed that when I let them slip, the harmful self-talk creeps back in.

That's not to say life is always 'perfect' and easy to navigate. Sometimes we must sit comfortably with bad feelings. Recognise them for what they are, for in those dark, uncomfortable times, real growth happens. We learn.

To truly grow, to move forward and towards our purpose, to love the now and look forward to our future with optimism, positivity and hope, I learned we must first believe and feel that the whole of ourselves is welcome. That our past doesn't define us.

We don't learn to sail in the calm sea, we learn to sail in the waves.

I've come to realise that when others make themselves vulnerable to us, and expose what they consider to be their flaws, we love them for who they are, flaws and all. Do we show ourselves the same compassion?

Do you feel ashamed of your reflection? I did. I'll be honest – I still do occasionally. But I know now the whole of me is enough. The whole of you is enough. It feels like a weight is lifted when you not only say those words, but really feel them to be true.

Occasionally, I will look back and regret decisions I have made, hurtful things I have said and done to people, those I have hurt or let down. I will beat myself up for wasting so many years hating myself and abusing my body.

But I have come to realise that I only think these things when I neglect myself day-to-day. So now I invest in myself, I love myself, and I show myself true care and compassion.

Forty ways to find YOUR freedom

Over the course of twelve months, after hitting rock bottom, I developed forty practical ways to heal myself. A list of #FortyTools to prescribe to myself day-to-day. Some are non-negotiable and part of my every day, like my bedtime routine, my ritual. What I used to see as a chore, I now consider a treat.

Others on the list, like igniting my senses on the beach, I sadly cannot do as part of my daily routine, as much as I would like to. But, wow, when I can, it has such a positive impact on my mental wellbeing. Just recognising that, and adding it to my armoury, is empowering.

Whether you find yourself in a place of adversity, or you simply recognise you could show yourself a little more self-love, I hope there are tools within this section that help you to grow, to find your purpose, to take you on a journey of discovery, and to make you feel energised.

Each of the #FortyTools has its own section. At first glance you'll be drawn to some over others. Don't fight that. Trust that your instinct knows what you need right here, right now.

This section doesn't need to be read end to end; think of it more as a medicine cabinet which you can dip into. I suggest having a glance through the section, highlighting parts that you're drawn to, but making a mental note of the others so you know they're there when you need them.

This is your book. This is your time for you. You're not expected to remember the contents of this book from cover to cover, so fold corners, write in the margins, highlight sections that resonate with you. Use *The Book I Wish I'd Read At 13* as your tool to unleash the true, free, version of you.

1) Rituals

Which parts of your day do you love the most? Think about it and write them down in a journal, perhaps.

Do you appreciate these times every day, or every time they happen? Or, more likely, do you do them on autopilot?

Here are mine:

- I love my first cup of tea in the morning, sitting on my own on the sofa at 05:00, under a blanket, before I read for sixty minutes.
- I love it when I see my children's faces for the first time each morning.
- I love it when my children come out of school each day and when Kit runs towards me with open arms and a huge smile.
- I love thirty minutes to myself each night when the house is sleeping. In silence, I cleanse, tone and moisturise my face. I spray my pillow with lavender sleep spray and rub a sleep balm into my temples. I lay on my bed with a wheat pillow over my eyes and listen to a guided meditation.

But I didn't used to fully appreciate these times.

I used to wake up, sit in bed for twenty minutes and scroll aimlessly through Facebook and Instagram, often drinking my tea without realising.

The kids would climb out of bed while I rushed around, preparing breakfast and getting uniforms ready. I'd jump in the shower, thinking of all the things I had to do before we left the house, rarely even looking the kids in the eye or saying a proper good morning.

At the school pick-up I'd be busy talking to other parents in the playground while saying a quick 'Hi' to Ted and Kit as they walked out of class. They'd ask what we had to eat at home and I'd have a quick flash of frustration and proclaim that was all they ever asked.

Most nights I'd go to bed without taking off my makeup, feeling grotty the next morning like I was still carrying with me the dirty parts of the day before.

Does any of this sound familiar?

Do you want to know the route to change, to contentment and love of the simplest things? The difference is being mindful, in the moment, in the 'now'. Appreciating what you're doing, seeing, hearing, feeling, touching, there and then, really tuning in to your body and your senses.

For me, it is looking at every tiny detail of the kids' faces as they sleep peacefully: their smooth skin, the varying shades of freckles on Ted's face, the length and curls of Kit's eye lashes, the softness of their lips. Witnessing their full smiles and giving them my absolute attention as they run out of class.

It is appreciating the kindness, the peace, the love I have for my own skin at bedtime. Taking the time to prepare my mind and body for a restful, energising and deserved sleep.

Be aware of the simple things you do each day that offer you the greatest pleasure. Be aware of where your mind is during those moments. Then see them as a ritual. A non-negotiable when your mind will be present.

It's had an incredibly positive impact on my day, and my sleep, when I've added one of these rituals to the start and end of my day.

Why not try it for yourself?

2) Being outside

Since Dad died, I've felt drawn to the outside, particularly the natural ground. I just can't explain it. Some mornings I will wander downstairs in my dressing gown and lay outside in the garden on a sun lounger with my morning cup of tea.

The vast, open beach feels like a sanctuary. The sound of the waves rolling and crashing was, and is, so therapeutic. Lying on the sand, whether it's the warm sand in Portugal or the cold spring sand in Norfolk, feels as good on my back and body as a treatment bed in a spa.

Playing football in an open field with Ted, opening my arms and chest and feeling the air in my lungs.

Sitting on the grass, I'll find myself stroking the green blades like they are soft feathers.

Listen to your mind and your body. Where do you feel drawn to? Follow your instinct and see where it leads you. Experience different versions of outside and tune in to your feelings. You'll soon notice how the outside makes you feel and I'm confident it will be a positive experience.

3) Drinking less alcohol

For some people this could perhaps be the most challenging tool on the list, but it's certainly helped me to feel better and think more clearly.

I've not been an excessive drinker since my mid-twenties, and even then, it was occasional binge drinking rather than regularly drinking to excess.

Since having the kids I've enjoyed drinking alcohol less and less. I don't like the thought of the kids feeling scared of their drunk parents. I don't like how it makes me feel the next day. It can take me a week to feel back on track and in a positive, healthy place.

Hangovers trigger me to binge eat.

Being over the drink drive limit scares me. I feel vulnerable and trapped if I can't get in the car in case of an emergency.

Alcohol turns me in to an idiot. I say things I don't mean. Drunk me is embarrassing. Or at least this is what I tell myself the next day. True or not, the self-talk isn't healthy.

I have kidney stones which are made worse by dehydration. I'm convinced my kidneys hate the alcohol so much that they make me vomit the stuff out of my body for most of the following day.

Alcohol gives you more confidence to fit in – that's my internal perspective. In reality, I stand out more for the wrong reasons; when I'm smashed, I act like a dick. Most people do.

The first drink is often lovely. The second is okay. After that, you don't even enjoy the drinks that much.

For a while now I've been thinking of making the bold statement: 'I don't drink.' But that first drink I really enjoy and what I'm trying to avoid is a life of rules.

So, I do drink, but I don't drink much. And on the rare occasion I do, I always regret it.

4) Mindful - social

Have you heard people say, 'I've come off Facebook for a while' or 'I'm limiting my time on Instagram to thirty minutes each day', or some other rule to live by, and break?

Unhealthy use of social media can make us feel rubbish about ourselves, take us off our path to freedom and make us think other people's paths are so much better than our own.

But what if we mindfully used social media, without rules? It doesn't have to be a negative place.

Next time you're scrolling, think about how a post makes you feel. Not just your first impression, but how it really makes you feel. If it brings up negative emotions of jealousy, self-hate or just makes you feel less than good, unfollow the account. It's as simple as that. And keep doing it until your feed contains nothing but positive, inspiring content.

Now, I tend to use Facebook to keep in touch with friends and family and Instagram for inspiration, blog posts and news from people that interest or inspire me, whether they're in the field of nutrition, wellbeing or just people doing positive things.

That said, even when the content is positive, if I find myself scrolling aimlessly, I will stop. It's like skim reading a book and not taking in half of the story – what's the point?

I think you'll find this is one of the #FortyTools that could have the quickest impact.

5) Popping bubbles

According to the Collins dictionary, the definition of *mindfulness* is:

NOUN

1.

the state or quality of being mindful

2.

the practice of giving complete and non-judgmental attention to one's present experience, used as a stress-reduction technique

But what happens when the mind is too full?

My final step to rock bottom felt exactly like that. That my mind was too full to see the wood through the trees. I had no mind space. No room to think about how to get the kids dressed for school. I felt a sense of overwhelm about the things I had to do, not just in the next ten minutes – getting the children to school – but my to-do list at work, the shopping I needed to get in the afternoon, the various pieces of life admin I needed to do for my family.

I was also spending a lot of time thinking about the things that had happened to me, and to us as a family. The bubble around me, my consciousness, was squeezed full of other bubbles of thought. I had no space left in my mind for anything else to fit in.

I had to hand some of those bubbles to other people, to share the responsibilities. I could no longer do everything for everyone else. I learned to delegate – something I've always found hard at work and at home.

Tom could get the shopping and do the washing. My friends could plan and organise the logistics of our nights out. It was a revelation that I didn't have to do everything for everyone else!

Some bubbles had to be popped, or at least placed in a cupboard for another time. I wrote in my diary things that I didn't need to think about for one week, one month or even one year into the future. My mind started to feel lighter. I could feel the air floating around inside my bubble, the gentle, slow, airy flow.

Awareness of the now helps me to focus. To still my thinking. To provide a sense of calm. To focus on the air instead of the bubbles.

You'll notice a thread throughout this section. Many of the tools I use day-to -day are based on the practice of being present, and aware of the now.

6) Meditation

My meditation practice is ever evolving, and it didn't start off intentionally. My first experience of meditation was when I was pregnant, and during my labour, with Kit. In contrast to my traumatic labour with Ted, I was determined Kit's arrival into this world would be more peaceful.

I delivered her without any pain relief, not even gas and air. I just meditated, making the vibrating sound of a humming bee through each contraction, taught to me by Tom's Auntie Janet, a yoga instructor.

My next experience of meditation wasn't until a few years later. Tina and I were sitting at Mum's bedside soon after her stroke. With little else to do, I read everything in sight, including her medical folder cover to cover, a few times over. I also scanned her diagnostics machine at sixty second internals, more so when something bleeped, which was often.

I had noticed the sensation of my heart racing and beating out of my chest regularly in the weeks after her stroke. I wondered what my heart rate was so I downloaded the 'Heart Rate Free' app on my phone. To my shock and horror my resting heart rate was averaging 115 beats per minute, when it should have been around 70 beats per minute.

I tried to relax, taking deep breaths and vowing to have a soak in the bath with some candles when I got home, which I did.

Climbing into bed, I recalled some guided meditations I had listened to during pregnancy yoga classes years earlier. I browsed YouTube and was excited to find some videos that I thought might help.

I laid in bed in the dark and played a guided meditation. I immediately felt my body softening and sinking into the mattress as I connected with my breath. It was blissful. The soft voice of the narrator, guiding me through a body scan or a tranquil visualisation, felt so instinctively wholesome and needed.

Quickly, I discovered the downside to listening to meditations on YouTube: when one video finishes, another begins. It became apparent that I couldn't fully relax during a meditation at bedtime as I had to stay fully awake in order to turn off my phone. Getting to sleep had been a real issue until discovering meditations, so I was determined to find a solution.

There are many smart phone apps that offer meditations – 'Calm' and 'Headspace' are just a couple. I use an app called 'Insight Timer'. Some apps are free, others offer a paid-for upgrade. Most will allow you to filter by length of meditation, turning off when finished. 'Insight Timer' also has free tools for kids, including bedtime stories, which are a great resource.

I've since moved on from the bedtime meditation, to a minimum of twenty minutes meditating, twice a day.

Meditation classes are now a staple part of my week. I love the whole experience: the smell, the soft lighting, the weight of the blanket and eye pillow over my body, lying on the mat, feeling my body sinking further and further in the ground inch by inch, feeling joints soften and muscles relax. It's almost a sensation of elongating each limb by 10% as the natural air in your fibres is freed.

These physical benefits are only trumped by the feeling of connecting with your breath, your body and allowing your mind to rest, to be still.

Meditation has been so transformative for me I've recently trained to teach meditation through The British School of Meditation, so I can share its benefits with others.

7) Yoga nidra

Yoga nidra, or yogic sleep as it is commonly known, is an immensely powerful meditation technique, and one of the easiest yoga practices to develop and maintain.

While the practitioner rests comfortably in *savasana* (corpse pose), this meditation takes you through the *pancha maya kosha* (five layers of self), leaving you with a sense of wholeness.

Yoga nidra is a practice that everyone, from children to seniors, can do. It's easy to follow at any age. All that your body needs to do is lie down on the floor. Even if you can't lie down on the floor, you can still do this practice seated.

As you lie down, all you must do is follow the voice that is guiding you. It's likely you will remember certain parts of the meditation and not others. Every time you come to the practice you encounter a new experience – none of which are wrong. Falling asleep is okay too, as you will still receive benefits while the unconscious mind is absorbing the practice.

Yoga nidra is always guided, so there is no intense thinking or wondering why you are staring at a blank wall. A yoga nidra practice can be as short as five minutes or as long as an hour.

You may find that the easiest way to accommodate a yoga nidra practice is to make it part of your daily bedtime routine. Put the headphones on, practice right in your bed, and then drift off to sleep. Although this is not the most conventional way to practice yoga nidra, you have no excuse not to do it if you're going to be lying down anyway.

Yoga nidra promotes deep rest and relaxation. The stages of body scan and breath awareness alone can be practiced, calming the nervous system, leading to less stress and better health.

Some people crave the profound relaxation that this practice instills, while other practitioners use the non-judgmental and secure atmosphere that yoga nidra provides as a window into themselves.

Yoga nidra offers a space to explore what you need in the moment, as well as an opportunity to work on releasing long-held emotions. During yoga nidra, you are able to experience an emotion and come 'face to face' with what you want to overcome, without 'diving into it' completely, meaning you won't feel the emotion so completely that you become overwhelmed.

Over time, you will continue to experience the emotion and associated feelings, moving deeper into the practice.

Yoga nidra is an accessible meditation practice that focuses on cultivating multiple levels of wellbeing. Practiced with consistency and awareness, you may likely discover that you can find a good amount of peace in a short period of time.

8) The freedom life

What does a life of freedom mean to you? Give yourself the time to really think about that question. Maybe find yourself a journal or notepad and jot down some words. They don't need to be organised into a sentence.

I thought about this for a very long time. The answer will be different for everyone.

Here is mine:

To have freedom to do what I want,
when I want, most of the time.

Freedom for me is not being accountable to anyone. Being able to sit and read a book for an hour after the school run, if that's what my mind and body needs, rather than having to clock-in at 09:00 and out at 17:00.

In the 'finding me' section I talk more about the freedom life, but just have it on your radar. Think about it when you're out for a walk or driving in the car. Your answers may change or develop but just go with your mind.

Work out what a freedom life would feel like to you.

9) Personal hygiene

One of the best things about going on holiday is the pampering sessions in the days before. Haircut and colour, nails painted, bikini line and forearms waxed, armpits free of hair, and perhaps even a relaxing cosmeceutical facial.

Who wouldn't feel great about themselves when they've been so looked after?

So why do we limit such luxury to special occasions and holidays? Why don't we show ourselves such care and attention all year round?

If my legs are hairy and I pull on a pair of jeans, it's like I can feel the friction reminding me to show myself some love.

Getting in bed with freshly brushed teeth and skin nourished from a skincare routine feels so incredible, much nicer than going to bed in the day's makeup and washing it off with shampoo the following morning – true story!

Give it a go, you'll thank me for it.

10) Say the words

If you love someone, tell them. One day you won't be able to.

Since losing my dad I feel so grateful that I always told him I loved him. It was so natural, so real. He instilled in me the ease with which I can say 'I love you' to my children. It's easy to just say the words but when you say them and think of the weight and depth of every word as they leave your lips, you feel deeply connected to the person receiving the love. Try it.

11) Connections

Sometimes I feel such overwhelming emotion for the people in my life.

When we talk about ourselves, not in a self-indulgent way but when we make ourselves vulnerable to others, we allow them to see it's okay for them to be vulnerable too.

It's when we're vulnerable that real connection is made.

Losing a parent is tough at any age. To experience such loss at 37 wasn't something I was expecting. But I was lucky. I have friends who lost their parents when they were still at primary school.

When we talk, we share, when we share, we grow.

I beat myself up for years that I wasn't the most popular at school. Throughout my teens I would calculate the hierarchy in our friendship groups and work out who was the most popular.

In the days, weeks and months that followed the loss of my dad, and our miscarriage, an army of friends were there for me. Checking in to see if I was okay, if I needed anything. I made countless trips to a local household store to buy more vases for the steady flow of flowers that arrived at my door.

It's when we're vulnerable that real connection is made. I felt it in abundance. Finally.

12) Journaling

I stumbled across this article by the University of Rochester Medical Center. Word for word, it explained journaling for mental health in such a perfect way, I decided to drop it in without editing:

When you were a teenager, you might have kept a diary hidden under your mattress. It was a place to confess your struggles and fears without judgement or punishment. It likely felt good to get all of those thoughts and feelings out of your head and down on paper. The world seemed clearer.

You may have stopped using a diary once you reached adulthood. But the concept and its benefits still apply.

Now it's called journaling. It's simply writing down your thoughts and feelings to understand them more clearly. And if you struggle with stress, depression or anxiety, keeping a journal is a great idea. It can help you gain control of your emotions and improve your mental health.

Journaling benefits

One of the ways to deal with any overwhelming emotion is to find a healthy way to express yourself. This makes a journal a helpful tool in managing your mental health.

Journaling can help you:

- *Manage anxiety*
- *Reduce stress*
- *Cope with depression*

Journaling helps control your symptoms and improve your mood by:

- *Helping you prioritize problems, fears and concerns*
- *Tracking any symptoms day-to-day so that you can recognise triggers and learn ways to better control them*
- *Providing an opportunity for positive self-talk and identifying negative thoughts and behaviours*

When you have a problem and you're stressed, keeping a journal can help you identify what's causing that stress or anxiety. Once you've identified your stressors, you can work on a plan to resolve the problems and reduce your stress.

Keep in mind that journaling is just one aspect of a healthy lifestyle for better managing stress, anxiety and mental health conditions. To get the most benefits, be sure you also:

- *Relax and meditate each day*
- *Eat a healthy, balanced diet*
- *Exercise regularly – get in some activity every day*
- *Treat yourself to plenty of sleep each night*
- *Stay away from alcohol and drugs*

Use your journal to make sure you follow these guidelines daily.

How to journal - try these tips to help you get started with journaling:

- ***Try to write every day.*** *Set aside a few minutes every day to write. This will help you to write in your journal regularly.*
- ***Make it easy.*** *Keep a pen and paper handy at all times. Then when you want to write down your thoughts, you can. You can also keep a journal in a computer file.*

- **Write whatever feels right.** *Your journal doesn't need to follow any certain structure. It's your own private place to discuss whatever you want. Let the words flow freely. Don't worry about spelling mistakes or what other people might think.*
- **Use your journal as you see fit.** *You don't have to share your journal with anyone. If you do want to share some of your thoughts with trusted friends and loved ones, you could show them parts of your journal.*

Keeping a journal helps you create order when your world feels like it's in chaos. You get to know yourself by revealing your most private fears, thoughts and feelings. Look at your writing time as personal relaxation time. It's a time when you can de-stress and wind down. Write in a place that's relaxing and soothing, maybe with a cup of tea. Look forward to your journaling time. And know that you're doing something good for your mind and body.

13) Reading

A friend asked me a question a few weeks ago: 'If you could do anything for a living, what would you do?'

It wasn't the first time I had been asked, and I'm sure you've been asked too. Perhaps you even ask yourself the question. I often do.

When I was younger, I would have said I wanted to be a PE teacher, then perhaps a hairdresser, or a makeup artist. For a while I may have even said a florist, despite having no talent in flower arranging. This time, when asked, I said, 'If I could do absolutely anything I would be paid to sit and meditate and read books all day.' And, my goodness, I meant it. I do hope that whatever the future holds, it involves sitting on the sofa and reading books for at least part of the day.

But it got me thinking – why do I love reading so much? Well, now I understand the answer(s). I love developing my mind, deepening my understanding of people and their minds, and allowing myself to grow and progress as a person.

But the main reason I love reading so much is it keeps me in the now. When I'm reading, I'm not worrying about the past or feeling anxious about the future. I'm in the now. I'm just being. Just me and a book. My mind is calm and still. And it's such a beautiful place to me.

Have you read *The Miracle Morning* by Hal Elrod? If you haven't, I thoroughly recommend it. It's a game changing book. At least it was for me, and I know it has been for many others.

Years before reading *The Miracle Morning* I would get up early – at 05:30 – to make a start on some work or read a book. It's a beautiful time to be awake, particularly in the summer. Listening to the birds singing, watching the sunrise, and seeing the changing colours of the dawn makes for a calm start to the day.

Since reading *The Miracle Morning*, I've added more structure to the extra hour I have before the rest of my family wakes up. I now insist on setting my alarm and rising for that extra hour, appreciating the benefits and seeing it as a luxury rather than a chore.

From 05:00-06:30 (depending on when my husband and children wake up), MY time is made up of meditation, visualisation, affirmation, yoga, reading and journaling. Some mornings I'll do more of one than the other. Often, reading will take up the largest chunk. Thankfully, I'm usually deep into a book that I just can't put down, which is why I tend to leave the reading until last.

Visit https://www.miraclemorning.com/ to find out more. You won't regret it.

14) Imperfection/perfection

I've wasted years of my life seeking validation from others. Telling myself I'd be more liked and accepted if I was thinner, prettier, more intelligent, had more expensive clothes or a high-paying job.

It's exhausting and, well, untrue.

For as long as I can remember, I've counted the rolls on my stomach and longed for a six-pack. Seriously, what a waste of life. Even at the times in my life when I was at my thinnest, I never actually appreciated the fact my stomach was flat, I just found something else to beat myself up about. I can even remember telling myself that when my stomach was flat it made my arms look fatter.

I can now honestly say I love myself for who I am today, who I was yesterday, and who I will become. Of course, I'm not perfect. What is 'perfect' anyway?

We all need to celebrate and love ourselves for everything we are, everything we have, everything we think, and everything we do. Life is too short to be any other way. The self-talk matters.

You might feel crazy doing it for the first time but try something. Find some space on your own, ideally by a window or a door, to let in daylight and be near the outdoors. Hold out your arms wide, stall tall, and say out loud, 'I love myself. I am enough!'

Try to do this every morning. It's a wonderful way to start the day and you never know, you may just start to believe it.

15) Awaken the senses

We all have times when we start to feel anxious. For whatever reason, panic starts to set in.

My husband who, for what it's worth, does not do deep, spiritual, mental health type chats – a typical alpha-male – had a panic attack in the car a few weeks ago. It was his first and took him by complete surprise. He's still trying to come up with a plausible reason for it.

My conclusion is that he was run down. He'd been out drinking too much, neglecting himself, and he was tired and caught up in the pre-Christmas hysteria.

I was driving and he said his heart was racing and he felt 'jittery' and 'weird'.

Without explaining to him what I was doing, I asked him to tell me about things he could smell, see, taste, touch and hear. Within a few minutes I watched him physically relax; his shoulders dropped, his head rested on his seat, his voice slowed.

By the time we arrived home, some fifteen minutes later, he felt better. I told him he could use that himself if he ever felt the same way again, or if he felt anxious, or even scared, in any situation.

Tuning in to your senses is a really simple way of bringing yourself back to the now. It's a tool I use all the time. It's also a beautiful way of appreciating the day-to-day. The fresh smell of flowers or clean washing, the sound of crashing waves or singing birds, the sight of a sunrise or sunset. Being present enough to appreciate all these simple things will always make you feel better.

16) Intuitive eating

As you will have read throughout this book, I've had a longstanding unhealthy relationship with food. I've lived by every rule and restriction there is. I could dedicate a whole book to intuitive eating and, who knows, I might one day.

Every single day we are exposed to brands that promote things we can spend our money on, to help us feel happier/better by losing weight. Once you can spot this and mindfully identify it for what is it – consumerism – you're half-way to winning the battle.

My journey to recovery has been an interesting one, non-typical I would say, having done it alone. It's been a longer, and perhaps tougher, path than if I had sought professional help. But I have learned so much about my eating disorder and how best to manage it.

It's tried to rear its ugly head a few times, often by trying to allow some form of rule to exist. There are many out there, here are just some, all of which I've found triggering:

- Vegan
- Vegetarian
- Extended fasting
- Liquid only
- Keto

I avoid labels. Sure, I now eat a plant-based diet. I don't particularly like meat and I was told by my urologist to avoid red meat because of my kidney stones. But I tell myself nothing is forbidden and it's so liberating! Instead, I focus on the delicious, healthy, varied, plant-based food I get to experiment with.

Nowadays I listen to how my mind and body feel after eating or drinking something. For example, I feel the slump soon after consuming sugar so I've concluded too much of it isn't good for me. But, crucially, I am led by what I enjoy and how things make me feel.

17) Date day

We spend all this time loving ourselves, working towards our vision and mission, caring for our children and carving out the career we've long dreamed of. I've learned it's easy to neglect your relationship with your partner, especially if you're in a long-term relationship.

I've been with my now husband for close to twenty-two years. Naturally, over the course of time, our relationship has changed from the rip-our-clothes-off early days. We've been through so much together and, to be honest, have taken each other for granted more than once.

I do struggle to be away from my children and, in truth, would always rather be with them than apart. But increasingly so, I'm appreciating the importance of making time to just be Kelly and Tom again.

We don't have the benefit of having my family near to us, only Tom's, so babysitters are limited, especially since Tom's siblings have all had children of their own. Because we've rarely used babysitters other than family, our children wouldn't be happy for us to pay a local babysitter to come and sit with them for an evening. And all those 05:00 starts mean that come 22:00 we're ready for bed.

Our weeks are filled with work, school, gym, yoga, football, gymnastics and trampolining duties. Tom and I have prioritised grabbing a few hours to ourselves when we can, at least once every few weeks, whether it's breakfast out or a trip to the cinema. Just time to chat and be us again feels so right and healthy.

18) Mindful spending

I never thought I could listen to my gut when spending money, but it's a thing.

I've come to realise that when I consider spending money on something extravagant, or unnecessary, my gut tells me it doesn't FEEL right.

Just recently, I was looking at a holiday for the four of us to the Maldives next Christmas. To be completely honest, I started looking after seeing influencers' stories all over Instagram while Tom and I sat at home after another lazy day on the sofa watching trash TV.

I had neglected the #FortyTools for a few days and was starting to feel the impact on my mental health.

Mindful spending doesn't just apply to the extreme of a £10,000 holiday to the Maldives.

When I've whizzed around a supermarket in a rush, paying no attention to prices and throwing in things we didn't need, I'd leave the checkout £70 lighter, the cupboards would still be bare, and I'd have the sinking feeling that I had wasted money.

In contrast, when I shop wisely, when I'm resourceful, I feel a sense of stability, a calmness. And it feels much better.

Listen to your gut. If you don't need it, and if it doesn't feel right, don't buy it, don't spend it. Look for the bargains; they **feel** much better.

19) Podcasts

I must admit, I was late to the podcast party, but what a discovery!

Most days I have at least thirty minutes to myself in the car. I've often had those trips where I'd get to my destination and couldn't recall most of the journey, after driving on autopilot. It's a worrying thought.

I would play music and not pay attention to it or listen to presenters and not really follow the conversation. I've even had journeys where the radio tuning was between stations and I would spend the whole trip listening to white noise, where I was anything but present.

Podcasts have changed all this.

In fact, I now look forward to each journey and see it as a chance to learn more, to discover other people and their experiences. I have learned so much about myself by listening to podcasts.

Some of my favourites are: *On Purpose* with Jay Shetty; *Happy Place* with Fearne Cotton; *The Naked Professors*; *How to Fail* with Elizabeth Day; *The Food Medic*; *No Really, I'm Fine*; and *Deliciously Ella*. I'm sure by the time this book is published I will have discovered a whole list more.

20) Music

Music does have its place too. Music is like a form of meditation; it can keep you in the present. But I do try to be mindful of how music makes me feel.

For example, the song 'Walk of Life' by Dire Straits was being played as I walked behind Dad's coffin into the crematorium. It's a fun song, a song I love, and we also played it at Dad's 50th birthday ten years before his funeral.

Often the song puts a smile on my face. Occasionally it makes me feel sad he's gone, but with a healthy level of grief. But sometimes the pain of grief hits too hard for me to sit with. These are the times when I have to turn off the song.

I love to sing along to Adele in the kitchen while making dinner, or to Kisstory during a hot afternoon in the garden. Music can be so uplifting and really change our mood for the better.

If we're mindful of how it makes us feel, it can be so therapeutic.

21) Faces

I remember the morning – it was the 25 March 2019. I know because I posted a picture of Kit on Instagram along with the following caption:

This morning Kit jumped in our bed for her morning cuddle, which she does every morning. More often than not I'm in a rush to get ready, to put on a load of washing, make the packed lunches, sort the school uniforms. This time I really cuddled her back without rushing, allowing all of my senses to enjoy those precious minutes. I really looked at her, taking in her long lashes, the growth of her 'big teeth', the gaps from her missing baby teeth, the curls of her hair. I smelt and felt her soft, clean skin. I wonder if by doing this every morning it will begin to feel less special. Well, I'm going to do it anyway. I wonder if big bro will let me do the same?

It was such a poignant moment.

Now, in the quiet moments when I'm lying or sitting with Tom, Ted or Kit, I'll take in their faces. The lines on Tom's face as he grows older, the freckles on Ted's face that reappear every summer, and Kit's face as she changes from a baby girl to our little girl.

I don't know why this makes me feel so warm inside.

Whether it's because it helps me to appreciate the now, or it's the flow of gratitude, it really does provide all the feels.

22) Trigger TV

Being mindful and being aware of how your mind (and body) feels in day-to-day situations helps to eliminate the stuff that makes you feel less than okay. I've come to realise some TV programmes cause me anxiety. I think in part it's because I'm an empath; I feel how the characters feel and I take on their emotions. It can be so stressful.

If you watched 'Cleaning Up', an ITV series aired early in 2019, you will have seen Sheridan Smith's character – a single mum and office cleaner – resort to insider trading to pay off her debts. I couldn't cope with watching her situation escalate out of control.

In my mind, TV should either be a form of escapism or educational in some way, it shouldn't trigger the negative emotions it can cause me.

I don't mean the producers or TV execs should change anything – for most viewers, 'Cleaning Up' wouldn't have had this effect.

The onus must be on us to be mindful of how TV programmes make us feel and adjust what we watch to protect our own mental health.

23) The 'no-blame game'

Listen out for how often you'll hear people, including yourself, blame others.

We can't control what other people do, say or think, but we can be mindful of the way we talk, including to ourselves. Since being mindful of blame, I've realised it's unhealthy, and has no advantage.

My husband Tom is guilty of this. I'm sure I am too sometimes. Once, he came back from the supermarket and forgot the washing tablets. I had reminded him to grab some as he walked out the door, but because they were not on the list I had written, he had forgotten.

Our conversation went something like this:

Me: (While putting the shopping away, and about to put on a load.) 'Did you grab the washing tablets?'

Tom: 'Oh s**t, I didn't. You didn't write them on the list, it's your fault.'

Me: 'Does it matter whose fault it was? We don't have them, so either you can go out to get some or I will.'

Tom: (Storms out the door.)

I must admit, even typing this conversation makes my fingers tense up with a little aggression! But it's true – does it really matter whose fault it was? Does pointing the finger of blame improve the situation, or make anyone feel better?

It's just as easy to blame ourselves for things but it's equally as pointless and useless.

24) Vision boards

If you're someway into your spiritual or personal development journey, you will have no doubt come across the concept of a vision board before now.

A vision board is what the name suggests: a visual collection of 'things' that make up your vision. It's usually a pin board, a photo-board or a combination of the two. Your vision board might include words/feelings, a home, car, holiday, children, a job, piles of cash or a yoga retreat. Your vision.

I have a vision board album on my phone and I scroll through it every morning, as part of my Miracle Morning. The key is not to just look at the photos but believe and feel they exist in your life already.

For example, on my vision board, I have a picture of a room in my future home which is a light and airy library with a comfy sofa. I feel myself lying on the sofa in the morning with my cup of tea, feeling the warmth of the sun on my back, a window open, letting in the sounds of the birds singing as I turn the pages of a great book. It's beautiful and serene.

Why not create your own?

25) Affirmations

Affirmations are positive statements that can help you to challenge and overcome self-sabotaging and negative thoughts. When you repeat them, often, and believe in them, you can start to make positive changes. Your affirmations might change over time, evolving as your life changes.

Here are my current affirmations, which I feel and repeat over and over each morning:

- I am fit, I am strong
- I am financially secure
- I have a large and connected following who I inspire to heal
- I am paid to write and paid to read
- My relationships are positive and healthy
- My children thrive and succeed and live a life full of happiness and confidence
- I live a freedom life
- Whatever I say, I am

Have a think about your own affirmations and write them down in a journal or notebook.

Like I say, they're ever evolving so there is no right and wrong, just be sure to keep them positive and in the first person.

26) Self talk

Say to yourself: 'I'm really scared, this is terrifying, I can't do it, I'm not good enough for this, I'm going to mess up. The world is such a dark and depressing place.'

See how it makes you feel. Check in to see what reaction this has caused to your physical being.

It makes me feel small, almost crouched down. My mood feels like it's slumping, like I'm starting to feel down about myself and unappreciative of my surroundings.

In contrast, say to yourself: 'What a bright and beautiful day. I love this life and the people I share the world with. I am so lucky to be holding this in my hands, to be on a path of self-discovery. I love myself and I AM enough.'

Now check in to see how you feel.

It makes me sit straighter and I welcome in the light from the window next to me. I generally feel more optimistic and brighter.

Just think, of all the people we share our lives with, we talk to ourselves the most. The negative talk will come; it's your ego trying to battle its way to the front of your mind. Check in regularly to see when the ego is talking and use your conscious mind to talk it back down. This does take some getting used to but keep with it.

Say you're about to give a presentation at work and you feel out of your comfort zone. In the minutes before you begin your heart may be racing, your stomach may be churning, and the ego will begin to tell you you're out of your depth, you're not good enough, you shouldn't be doing this. Mindfully say to yourself, 'This is just nerves talking. It's healthy to be nervous, it's my body giving me the positive energy it needs to do a good job. I know the subject I am talking about and people want to hear what I have to say. I am enough.'

Be aware of how you are talking to yourself and make a conscious decision to use kinder language.

27) Touching

As well as emotional connections, we all need physical connections to make us feel well, and alive. It's one of the most important parts of human life, right from the beginning of life, when babies need to cry, suckle and cling to their parents for survival, and to create a bond.

I see the positive impact a gentle hand on the head has on my children as they enter their classroom each morning. And a 'pat on the back' makes us all feel like we've done well and that we're valued.

Oxytocin is released into the body upon physical touch, such as cuddling. Oxytocin can counter the effects of cortisol, the stress hormone. The wonder hormone helps us connect to others and promotes a good feeling and a sense of happiness.

My kids will probably tell you they're sick of me cuddling them. In fact, Kit wouldn't – she still loves a cuddle at every chance. Ted, at the tender age of 10, often shies away from an embrace with his mum. When he wakes every morning, he'll still climb into our bed, just for a few seconds for a tired squeeze. Those few seconds I treasure. I know we're all benefiting from the warmth of each other's touch.

Before the children came along, Tom and I would lay in each other's arms every evening, watching a film. Every morning we'd wake up and hug before our mornings began. The number of times we've got to do this over the past five years I can probably count on one hand, but we'll grab a quick hug in the kitchen while the kettle is boiling, or in the morning as he leaves for work.

I think quality is as important as quantity when it comes to cuddles. Five seconds, in the moment, taking in the flow from all my senses, feels so special. But it doesn't need to be a touch from your children, or your husband. Of course, I'm not suggesting you go around squeezing strangers, but hug your friends, put an arm around your niece or nephew as they show you their latest toys. Everyone will feel the benefits.

28) Feeling your flow

What is it you do, that you get completely lost in, where you lose all track of time? For me, it's reading, or writing. Or even playing around with my (huge) collection of makeup.

But it could be exercising, playing the piano, painting or something else creative. It might not easily come to mind. But there will be something.

I could easily spend eight hours straight sitting on the sofa with a great book. Rarely would a random thought spring to mind.

When you're completely in the flow of something you love – truly love – you will be entirely present. In the moment. You cannot be depressed or anxious when you are in your flow.

Quite often it feels like a luxury, or a waste of precious time, to be doing these things. But when you realise they have such healing benefits, you'll appreciate they need to be a priority. Find the thing that is your flow and make the time for it.

29) Reflective healing

I bet you've used the phrase 'I really should listen to my own advice' or words to that effect. Subconsciously we all do.

Since I've been on the path of post-traumatic growth, since I've made myself vulnerable, I've been like a magnet to other people sharing their problems and concerns. I've realised that every person I've offered advice to, listened to, thought about and mentored, has helped me to further heal too.

Emotional intelligence, spirituality, self-help, personal development, however we want to define it, really is the gift that keeps on giving.

I remember, some time ago, before I started to put pen to paper, before this book was even an idea, I had no idea what I wanted to do. I just remember saying to someone, 'I just feel like I want to heal people.' To be honest, at the time, I wasn't in a great place myself, so the notion that I was looking outward instead of inward took me by surprise. But it was that determination, motivation and desire to eventually help others that helped me bring myself far enough along to put it into practice.

Witnessing other people's vulnerabilities, letting them share their problems and worries, makes you realise you are not alone. Although the pendulum of support might currently swing to them, you never know when it might start to swing back, and those real connections will better support everyone involved.

30) Girl power

I've not spoken too much about my friends in this book. It wasn't a conscious decision but my handful of best friends, who I have a deep, lifelong connection with… Well, quite simply, I cannot put into words the love I have for them. I need them.

Tasha

I phone her most days at 14.40 when I jump in the car on my way home from work. There is nothing I wouldn't share with her. Although saying that, I've never spoken about my long-term eating disorder with her, but something tells me it won't come as a surprise.

I love this girl. On my deathbed I will be so thankful I got to spend my life with her. We were each other's bridesmaids. Most years we'll holiday together with our families. She was with me in Portugal when I had the call to say my mum had suffered a stroke.

She came with me to hospital when I miscarried. We've shared the ups and downs.

She's not so into all this 'wanky, deep shit' and would probably cringe and tell me to 'bore off' if I told her I was writing these words about her.

She's the life and soul of the party. Always the last to bed on a girl's holiday or a night out, of which there have been many.

She's fit and emotionally and physically strong. I tell everyone she ran the London Marathon with a broken foot. I think I've exaggerated the story over the years but she really is a gladiator in my mind.

If I haven't made it clear enough, I love this girl!

Vicky

Vicky is Tasha's sister. There is just over one year between them. It would usually be difficult, I guess, being best friends with two sisters, but it never has been. As far as I'm aware, no one has ever felt left out or cast aside.

Tasha and Vicky are so similar in many ways. They both belong on the cover of *Sports Illustrated* magazine but personality-wise their only similarity is they can both party until the early hours!

Vicky has the best laugh I've ever heard; a proper belly chuckle. I can laugh just at the thought of her laugh.

She's tactile, funny, warm, silly and beautiful. She just brightens my day and I am so thankful to have her in my life.

Anna

Mrs Bendall – Deputy Director of Sixth Form and a teacher of business at a local, high-performing school. She's the clever one in the group.

She's also one of the people I connect with most when it comes to the deep, spiritual stuff.

But, my goodness, she's also crazy! She's hilarious and so much fun. We have had endless, tummy-aching laughs at Anna's expense!

She has the quickest of wits, a brilliant dry humour. Her legs go on forever. She is incredibly beautiful with a body to die for. Beauty, intelligence, loyalty and sass she has by the bucket load, but sadly she can only see those traits in us.

She's nearly always my roomie and I've seen her naked arse more times than I can remember! I adore her, more than she probably realises. My life would be incomplete without her.

Lisa

Lisa was the first person I told about this book. She was the first to read the manuscript.

She's the person in my life I feel least nervous about baring all too. That speaks volumes about the level of connection we have. I cherish our friendship and love her dearly.

She's a free spirit. I'd say she's the only person in my life who is as deep as me. We have many shared passions: writing, 'proper' books, print, pouring out our hearts, and we both have an endless supply of love to give.

She's super stylish, a professional shopper. Well, actually, she's an editor but she should be a professional shopper. She has more hats and accessories than I have of anything.

We lived out of each other's pockets for many years, from our early twenties. A few years ago Lisa moved to a new house and now lives a couple of hours away, so we don't see each other as much as I would like. I miss her. In fact, I'm going to tell her that now. There is no time like the present.

Lisa has had her own fair share of stuff to deal with over the last few years and I regret that I've not been there for her as much as I would have liked.

I trust the universe to do its thing and I feel confident we'll be back to living out of each other's pockets again soon.

I asked her what I should write about her in this section and she said, 'Small. That's kinda all I have.' Small she is, with the biggest heart you'll find.

And those four are the core of my girl gang. The girls I could never be without. All so different but together we make up something priceless. We've been friends for close to thirty years. Thirty years! That's a long time. Even more so for Tasha and Lisa whose birthdays are three days apart – their mums were in hospital together. And of course, Tasha and Vicky who are sisters.

These girls have helped me to understand and love myself. Tasha, Vicky, Anna, Lisa, I love you. I look forward to our lives together.

If I could grant the world one wish, it would be for everyone to have the gift of true friendship that you have all given me.

31) Psychotherapy

For those in present or post trauma, the prospect of mindfulness, which is at the core of many of the #FortyTools, could be a gateway to a mind full of traumatic stress.

If this is the case, or if you have had thoughts of suicide, it would be beneficial to seek professional support.

This book is by no means a replacement for professional help.

I've included a directory of places at the back, to go for extra support. I got it. I know it's daunting to ask for help especially if, like me, you've been putting on a brave face and 'functioning' for a long time.

I promise you, once you've said those first words it's much easier to move forward.

Before I went to my GP I played over and over the first words I was going to say, to explain how I was feeling. I even had a note on my phone, a script. But, as soon as I sat in front of my GP, everything I planned to say fell to one side. I cried and said, 'I just feel so overwhelmed.'

Instantly, a weight was lifted.

Just tell one person. That's all it takes to find your path. The taboo of mental illness is slowly diminishing and that's because more and more people are talking about their own experiences.

Be brave.

Start talking.

32) Money management

Money worries are the worst. Not knowing how you're going to pay the bills can literally keep you up at night, and I'm sure most of us have had times when we've lived beyond our means.

I've read many stories of people, especially men, who have ended their lives because of the weight of debt on their mind. What a waste.

While working for homeless charity Emmaus UK, I heard the phrase: 'Most of us are only three pay days away from homelessness.'

That's scary.

There was a time in my life, not too long ago, when I begrudged paying bills. I had much 'better' things to be spending money on. But then I consciously changed my mindset.

Tom and I have our health, which means we can go out to work and earn the money to pay our bills. We do not live a life of luxury, but our children don't go without. Our lives are fun, we go on lots of adventures, and we have a clean, warm home.

For now, we must take pleasure in the fact we're able to live a full life within our means, and believe that the financial freedom will come.

33) Work addiction

In the summer before Dad died, I was working for an international events agency. In the month before an event I was working eighty hours a week, from home, with a young family. It wasn't ideal.

I took on another job and didn't know how to turn off the work switch. Often, I would work until 22:00, or sometimes 02:00 or 03:00, to meet deadlines.

I was running on adrenaline. If I wasn't working, either in traditional work or jobs around the house, I didn't know what to do with my time. I couldn't just *be*.

The only other time I felt such an addiction to work was when I was six months pregnant with Kit. I was working at Emmaus UK, and we'd been through a restructure. I told myself I couldn't start maternity leave until I had recruited and trained a new team. Every time I sat at my desk I would get heart palpitations, but I just couldn't stop working. It was all I could think to do.

The midwife referred me to the GP who wanted to sign me off work with stress. I begged him not to, stating that the stress of knowing all the stuff I needed to do at work would cause me even more stress.

I wish I knew then what I know now. I wish I'd had the #FortyTools in my armoury, to carve time out for myself, to be calm and still. To just *be*.

Work addiction is sometimes hard to spot. It may not be something you're experiencing right now but just be mindful it's a thing. And an unhealthy thing at that.

Take the time to quash it if you need to, because you're much more important than work.

34) Toilet time

There have been times in my life when I've been too busy to go to the toilet (see 'work addiction' above). So much so that I've given myself water infections from holding in a wee for too long.

If you're a mum, and especially if you're a new mum, you might feel like you don't get the chance to go to the toilet without interruption. When Ted was a newborn I used to take him to the bathroom with me in his Moses basket!

But (assuming your baby is safe) what can't wait for two minutes?!

Sure, there will be times when you just need a quick wee but, let's face it, sometimes you'll need more than a quick wee!

Instead of taking your phone with you to have a quick scroll through Facebook, whilst sitting on the pan with nothing to do, give yourself time to take some good, quality breaths.

Slow your breathing. Breathe in for four, out for four, pause for four, and then in for four, out for four, pause for four. Sit with this exercise for a few minutes. You'll feel much calmer and better prepared for whatever task you're faced with next.

35) Time to cry

My kids often see me cry. I cry at the TV, even adverts. I cry during football matches when I see the losing team cry. I cry at applause and my kids' assemblies. Happy tears, sad tears. Lots of tears.

Kit looks concerned whenever she sees me cry. If there is something sad on the TV, she'll look straight at me with panic on her face, to see if I am crying. I don't like it. I feel guilty that she worries about me at her tender age of 6. But I do want them to know it's fine to cry. That it's an emotion just like happiness, anger, frustration and joy.

Sometimes I see them holding back the tears and I'll ask, 'Do you need a cry?' Then their tears will flow. I do wonder why it's an emotion we're often too embarrassed to show. I think we should embrace it and let those tears flow.

Who doesn't feel better after a good cry?

36) Routines

Holidays, Christmas, Easter, time off school – they're all wonderful, special times, but for a long time I struggled as they left me craving routine. Often during these times, without realising, we feel out of sorts because we've neglected the things that make us feel good. Whether that might be exercise, our usual diet, enough sleep, journaling, or time for ourselves.

Just recently, during these times and holidays, I've tried to keep to some routine whether that be sleep and awake times, movement, reading, or taking time for general self-love or the #FortyTools, and I've felt so much better for it!

Work out the non-negotiables in your day and see if you can include them when your normal routines change.

37) Boundaries

Sometimes, however much we invest in ourselves, our environment and the people around us, there will always be someone or something that works against us. Whether that be a person, a job, or an environment. It's our responsibility to take ownership of our own lives and wellbeing.

There are some accounts I used to follow on Instagram that, time and time again, made me feel crap about myself.

I could never change the content that person shared, despite leaving a few comments explaining the post was triggering for people with eating disorders. So, I took ownership and unfollowed the account.

There is a soft play centre local to us where my children or their friends would leave with a cut or bump every time we visited. When my anxiety was at its peak I would start to panic as soon as we got in the car to go. I had to give it a miss for a few months or else I would have passed on my anxiety to my children.

There are people in my life who, for whatever reason, make me feel bad about myself. Not often consciously or through fault of their own, but I keep them at arm's length. If I'm not going to prioritise myself in my own life, who will?!

To protect yourself, put up the boundaries you need to live a full, happy and content life.

How true were the words spoken by Iris (played by Kate Winslet) in the film 'The Holiday': 'You're so right. You're supposed to be the leading lady of your own life, for god's sake.'

38) Look into the clouds

This is something Tom and I did on one of our first dates and it's something that you're nearly always able to do.

Whether you're walking home from the school run, sitting at your desk, or in the car as you pull up to work, look up to the sky, almost through the clouds. What do you see? Clouds moving in the wind, various shades of grey or bright blue, or even a hazy moon? You can't help but feel a tiny part of something so big, such an expanse. But you also feel still in a moving world.

Just sit and be, taking in what you see. Relax your breath and you'll begin to feel present.

39) Colouring

I stumbled across this by chance. I had seen shelves of grown-up colouring books and, to be honest, dismissed the idea.

But Kit received some new colouring pens for her birthday and asked me to fill in the left-hand page while she did the right. I'm not arty, although I loved life drawing classes at college. But colouring is my new-found joy!

Choosing the nicest colours and the challenge of keeping inside the lines is something I find so relaxing and therapeutic. It's easy to get 'lost in the flow' and it's something that Kit and I love to do together. It's even occurred to me to get Ted involved; I can see how it will benefit him during his fast approaching, hormonal, teenage years.

Try it, we love it.

40) Trust the universe

As much as we can document our visions, write our affirmations and create a life plan, the simple truth is that we do not know what the future holds.

We have to sit comfortably with the thought that the road ahead will be great, full of love and happiness, but it will also be bumpy at times.

Let's take a breath, buckle up, embrace all those around us and enjoy the ride of life that the universe offers us.

From adversity, I have found real strength. Post trauma, I have grown. I hope that by adopting some of the #FortyTools you feel better equipped for your journey.

Post your photos on social media with the hashtag #FortyTools – let's inspire others to show themselves the love they deserve too.

Becoming Me

Freedom life

I wrote *The Book I Wish I'd Read at 13* as a way of baring all. Sharing the 'secrets and shame' I've held inside for close to forty years. The self-harming was damaging and I needed to free myself, to live my life, for my children but also for myself.

I don't recall where I first heard the term 'freedom life' but I soon understood what a life of freedom would mean for me:

> *To have freedom to do what I want,*
> *when I want, most of the time.*

I needed this thing called a freedom life.

On the surface, this makes me sound like I am spoilt or materialistic but bear with me.

Through extensive reading, investment in the #FortyTools, and listening to a library of podcasts, I have developed self-awareness by the bucket load.

So, what have I learned about myself?

- I am an introvert.
- I prefer to not be in big groups.
- I recharge by sitting in silence, reading a book.
- I prefer intimate conversations, real connections, either one-to-ones or in small groups, over the complicated chatter of large groups.
- I like to work at home on my own, in silence, rather than in an energetic, fast-paced office.
- There are times when I feel highly productive and motivated. At other times I just need to be still and clear my mind. To be. Sometimes I work best during the day, sometimes it's at 20:00.

Why?

Because I'm an empath. I feel people's emotions, their energy, their moods like they're my own. I'm a 'highly sensitive person' (HSP).

A HSP is identifiable by the following:

- Being overwhelmed by sensory stimuli like noisy crowds, bright lights or uncomfortable clothing.
- Feeling the need to avoid violent movies or TV shows because they feel too intense and leave you feeling unsettled.
- Feeling not just a preference but a *need* for downtime, to retreat to a dark, quiet room, especially when you have hectic days.
- Being deeply moved by beauty, either expressed in art, nature or the human spirit, or sometimes even a good advert.
- Having a rich and complex inner life, complete with deep thoughts and strong feelings that go with it.

When I read the list of traits of an empath or a HSP it was like I discovered myself for the first time. 'Yes, yes, yes!!! This is me!!!' I wanted to shout.

Perhaps you can identify with some of these traits too?

On my journey of self-discovery, whilst chatting with Mum, she told me something about my younger self. As a child, if we were walking along the street and a neighbour was cutting their grass,

I would cover my ears. I hated the sound of the lawnmower. I would force my mum to cross the road with me to escape the torture.

Likewise, I couldn't stand the noise of a busy hairdressers, with all the hairdryers playing in chorus. This explains why I go to Val, in a gorgeous little hair salon in Great Dunmow, with one seat and one hairdryer and the chance to have a real conversation with deep connection.

By recognising these traits, I started to understand why I love the things I love and which environments I feel most comfortable in. And, on the flip side, why some things just don't fit right with me. And that's fine.

It's not wrong to not be like other people and to not like the same things as them. It was an awakening and a relief to realise something so simple.

It's okay that I cringe with awkwardness when my extrovert friends drag me up to dance on a stage! And why I feel overwhelmed in a busy office.

Society – 'normal life' – works against these traits. Often, we're expected to work in a busy office from 09:00-17:00 and perform at our best during these hours. I have known for some time that this isn't how I work best. But now I understand why.

Understanding the why, understanding what doesn't work for our personality type, helps us to carve out the life that does fit well with our traits, likes and desires.

It helps us to create our 'freedom life'.

To have freedom to do what I want,
when I want, most of the time.

When we think about what we do, our first thought is often our job, our career.

I worked for many years for Emmaus UK. People who were homeless would often tell me one of the things they found most tough was not having an answer to the question, 'What do you do?'

Our job helps us to feel validated. Not only does it provide a salary to enable us to pay our bills, but it gives us a purpose.

Since having Kit in 2013, I spent close to seven years feeling I wasn't on the right path. As you've learned, by hitting rock bottom and investing in myself through the #FortyTools, I've changed the course of my life.

While writing this book I am still working in fundraising, but in many ways I'm clearing a new path.

These are the things I want, things I will manifest:

- I will show Ted and Kit the world. Light up their senses by seeing the beauty the world has to offer. Let them see and feel the sand on stunning white beaches. Experience different cultures and meet people whose experiences, values and beliefs are different to their own.
- I will drive around in a car that's safe and comfortable, with a boot big enough to carry multiple pairs of muddy football boots, wellies, winter coats, and a bag of reading books.
- I will have a warm, welcoming home where we can entertain and enjoy special times with family and friends.
- I will have an office with bookshelves, housing my own books and others, with a sofa where I can lay with a blanket, light some candles, and enjoy a peaceful read.
- I will have a kitchen where I'll play soft music as I prepare dinner for our family, with a cosy dog basket, home to a red-haired cockapoo.
- I will have a small room dedicated to recording podcasts.
- I will have a light and bright space where I can meditate and practice yoga, big enough for friends and clients to join me.

In the interest of transparency, I'd also quite like a walk-in wardrobe stocked with crisp white clothes and comfy activewear. I almost held back from writing this, feeling that it was indulgent, but it's on my vision board so I must commit to sharing my vision with you, and with the universe.

To be honest, I don't want for much more than that. Other than good health, of course. But, thanks to my own experiences, that's something I now never take for granted.

What does a freedom life look like to you? You won't come up with all the answers now but regularly ask yourself the question. Grab yourself a notepad – a nice one – and start to write down the answer.

You will have read sections on journaling, vision boards and affirmations in the #FortyTools, so I hope you're starting to build a picture of what you want to bring to your own life.

Plans for the future

My plan is to be a positive influence on as many lives as possible through a large and connected following. I've recently trained as a meditation teacher with The British School of Meditation, and I have just begun my two hundred hour yoga teacher training in the Apanaveda style of yoga, which is a slow but strong practice of yoga where the breath initiates and inspires all movement.

The #FortyTools, individually, are not unique. However, combined and documented as a resource, I believe they are invaluable to other mums and, in fact, *all* women and young girls.

Soon after this book hits the shelves (which must have happened for you to be reading it!), I will have launched, or will soon be launching, my own meditation classes.

There are many courses that I'm considering. I've spent days, probably months, unhealthily overthinking which ones to do first. I'm taking a step back and focusing on this book while I let the universe figure out what's next for me.

Only the universe knows what other exciting things it has planned.

I have a few other ideas, including some work dedicated to eating disorder campaigning. Recently, I heard the outrageous idea all over the press that food labels should include the exercise time required to burn off the calories contained. I can only hope by the time this book is published this has not come into force.

Recently, I listened to *The Naked Professors* podcast with Sam Thompson, who discussed the idea of #edited being used on all social media images if the photo has been edited or photoshopped. This is something that just MUST happen, and I would love to support this campaign.

Body image is an increasing problem for young people, and those not so young, I guess. It was a huge problem for me growing up and I wasn't faced with the social pressures that exist today.

As you will have read, my unhealthy relationship with food played a huge part in my life for many years. It was a form of self-harm.

I chose to punish myself, subconsciously, for not being enough. It breaks my heart that so many women (and men) are doing the same. In my mind, it's more common than people think and I believe it's part of the reason the western world has an obesity crisis. I didn't binge because I loved food and it wasn't as straightforward as just eating less.

I'd like to write a book about intuitive eating, using food as a barrier to self-love. Maybe that will come next, who knows?

I'm also keen to write a book for teenagers, called *The Book I Wish All Teens Could Have*. A book for a parent to buy their child, to read first and share. A conversation starter. There were so many conversations I wish I had had with Mum, but I couldn't find the words.

The Book I Wish All Teens Could Have would stress to every parent the importance of trust and confidence. *The Book I Wish All Teens Could Have* may include a resource, maybe cue cards, for a child to use to start difficult conversations by leaving a note under their pillow for their mum, dad, or guardian to see.

The note might read: *I feel lonely*, or *I've started my period*, or *I'm developing an unhealthy relationship with food*, or even *I've been abused*. Girls (or even boys) and their parents need to be having these conversations, to prevent lives wasted under the dark cloud of shame.

Someone once said to me I should write a book that I wish I had read. I want to tell all children, all young people, that they are enough, that they belong, that they should feel no shame. I want everyone to feel they have at least one person they can talk to.

I've loved the process of writing *The Book I Wish I'd Read At 13*. It's helped me understand so much about myself. I can't turn back time and I'm not sure I would if I could. But I do hope, from the deepest place within me, that through this book I can help other women to heal themselves from their past, help children to feel they belong, and open the eyes of mums with teenage girls to some of the emotions their daughters may be battling with.

My purpose

What I do know is my purpose is to help others.

One of my favourite quotes is:

> *'The final stage of healing is using what happens to you to help other people.'*
> Gloria Steinem

I couldn't have said it better. This quote perfectly articulates my purpose.

My purpose is to help others, particularly mothers, to find and love the real them. To open themselves up, to understand themselves deep to their core, and to unleash their true potential.

What was my original motivation to take myself on this journey – was it for me or my children? Did I intentionally take myself on this journey?

Both of those questions I find it difficult to answer. I don't recall ever consciously deciding to do all those things listed in the #FortyTools.

Did I find them or did they find me? I'm not sure. I certainly didn't ever think I would be writing a book about my own experiences.

Many of you will be familiar with post-traumatic stress disorder (PTSD) but have you heard of post-traumatic growth (PTG)? It's a thing. And I'm living it.

I've said before that by losing my dad and mum I've been able to find myself. What an incredible legacy they were able to leave their child.

I really hope that by writing and publishing this book I can help other women to move along this journey of self-discovery, and to find it as enlightening and life-changing as I have, and still do.

Whether I found myself for myself or for my children, I don't know, but the positive impact has been felt by all of us. In fact, by all those around me.

I hope you have taken something from *The Book I Wish I'd Read At 13*, something that helps you on your path to a freedom life.

Free of the weight of the past.

Free of self-inflicted pain.

Free of unreasonable expectations.

I hope you will find the time to prioritise you. To finding the real YOU.

Much love.

Help Directory

References, podcasts and further reading

'By Kelly Oakes' is a hub for all things meditation, breathing and yoga. As well as online and studio classes, you'll find products for sale which will help you embed the #FortyTools in your day-to-day life.

www.by-kellyoakes.com

As well as my own website and social media channels, you may find the following resources of interest too:

My favourite podcasts

On Purpose with Jay Shetty

Happy Place with Fearne Cotton

The Naked Professors

Under The Skin with Russell Brand

How to Fail with Elizabeth Day

The Food Medic

No Really, I'm Fine

Deliciously Ella

Further reading

The list of books I love is too long to include in this book, and there isn't a 'one size fits all' book. Take a look at my Instagram for book reviews and recommendations based on various subjects, such as living with an eating disorder, mindset, meditation and personal development.

References

Journaling for Mental Health by University of Rochester Medical Center

https://www.urmc.rochester.edu/encyclopedia/content.aspx?ContentID=4552&ContentTypeID=1

Supermarket Flowers by Ed Sheeran

https://www.edsheeran.com/

The Miracle Morning by Hal Elrod

https://miraclemorning.com/

Directory of places to go for help

Rather than add a long list here, these are places I've personally used or visited:

www.counselling-directory.org.uk/ – an online directory of counsellors.

https://happiful.com/ – an online magazine for all things related to mental health and wellbeing.

www.youngminds.org.uk – the UK's leading charity dedicated to children and young people's mental health.

www.anorexiabulimiacare.org and www. beateatingdisorders.org.uk – both UK charities with helpline services for people with an eating disorder, and their families.

www.teaching-meditation.co.uk – The British School of Meditation, to find a teacher near you.